T3-BNR-717

A SHORT VIEW
OF THE ENGLISH STAGE
1900–1926

A SHORT VIEW
OF THE
ENGLISH STAGE
1900–1926

BY
JAMES AGATE

BENJAMIN BLOM
New York/London

To
LEWIS CASSON
AND
SYBIL THORNDIKE

First Published 1926
Reissued 1969 by
Benjamin Blom, Inc., Bronx, New York 10452
and 56 Doughty Street, London, W.C. 1

Library of Congress Catalog Card Number 75-91887

Printed in U.S.A. by
NOBLE OFFSET PRINTERS, INC.
NEW YORK 3, N. Y.

NOTE

THAT which follows is not an essay in dramatic criticism, and no highly-coloured descriptions of plays or players will be presented. The object of the writer is less to present facts than to trace causes and deduce something of effects. That which is deduced is that though some things may be rotten in Elsinore all is well with Denmark. And perhaps Elsinore is not in quite so poor a way as a casual inspection of Rosencrantz Avenue and Yorick Circus might suggest. Nothing will be said about the decline of the great actor and the rise in general level of accomplishment among players, neither are the questions of scenery and production touched upon, the excuse being the old one of the quart and the pint-pot. For other omissions due to ignorance or forgetfulness the writer craves pardon.

CONTENTS

CONTENTS

A SHORT VIEW OF THE ENGLISH STAGE

TWO STANDARDS

IN attempting what must necessarily be a bird's-eye view of the history of the English stage during the past twenty-five years it is necessary to make a distinction between the drama and the theatre. The drama is an æsthetic phenomenon, the theatre is an economic proposition. The two things have little in common, though your theatrical manager confounds them easily enough. The late William Archer laid it down that there are three rules, conformity to which entitles us to look upon a play as a great play. The rules may conveniently be put in the form of questions. Does a play present a reasonable and faithful imitation of the visible and audible surfaces of life, without intrusion or caricature, or shiftings from one plane of convention to another? Is the story developed, and are the characters presented, in such a way as to make the best use of the mechanism of the theatre, and to beget in the audience emotions of growing interest, suspense, anticipation, sudden and vivid realisation? I should be inclined to paraphrase this by asking: Is the spectator all agog to know what A will do next, and what B will answer to C? The third and last question is: In seeing this play have we not merely enjoyed a pastime, but undergone an experience? From the point of view of the critic a play is a great play which answers these questions successfully. But the only criticism of which the theatre-manager takes stock is his weekly box office returns. "Great, my boy, great!" he will say, rubbing his hands over some piece of imbecility which has played to capacity; whereas the thinnish stalls and empty dress-circle, which are the reward of Ibsen and Tchehov, will set him talking of "dud shows." Yet the æsthetic value of a piece obviously remains constant whether three people pay to see it or three thousand.

The amount of money taken by the box office represents the number of people who have forked out hard-earned cash to see something which they think they will enjoy, and it is an old tag that there are as many shades of opinion as there are individuals. In other words, "everybody" means all kinds of anybody. Mrs. Brown after a day of slaughter at the Summer Sales may like wetting six pocket-handkerchiefs to see a young woman climb Ludgate Hill in bare feet and a snowstorm, with one or more infants clasped to her breast. The point to be decided is whether *Driven from Home* is, or is not, a good example of its kind. Elderly Mr. Robinson, who knows Russia in so far as he once represented a firm of sewing machine makers in that country, may enjoy a piece in which a flighty, middle-aged woman is told that if she doesn't take steps to pay off a mortgage, the mortgagee will foreclose. She doesn't take those steps, and the nasty fellow —all mortgagees are nasty fellows—does foreclose. One agrees with Mr. Robinson in thinking *The Cherry Orchard* a great play, because the play is good of its kind, and because the kind is great. And the playgoer who does not wish to judge foolishly will avoid saying that he doesn't like *The Cherry Orchard* because he adores *Driven from Home*, or vice-versa.

AVAUNT REALISM!

One of the factors with which we have to reckon is that to the vast majority of playgoers the theatre is a world of make-believe. The average playgoer does not want realism. He does not want, on the stage, a picture of the life he knows. Mr. St. John Ervine once wrote a play called *Jane Clegg*, which was all about an exasperating, well-meaning young woman who was married to a not very well-intentioned commercial traveller. It was an exceedingly fine play. Now who were the people who went to see it? Did the commercial travellers take their wives? No. Did the Jane Cleggs take their Henrys? No. The people who went to see it were the intellectual folk who have travelled in every way except the commercial. It is the poor who help the poor. Agreed. But the poor are satisfied with helping; they don't want to see serious plays about those of their number to whom they have just slipped a couple of bob. I am not going to maintain that very many of the rich like plays about the poor. They also like plays about the well-to-do. There are, I suppose, a thousand commercial travellers' wives to every lady of title. None of these wives wants to see a play about one of her kind stealing with all her pitiful little belongings out of Henry Clegg's house for the best of reasons. What she wants to see is your high-born lady—and what that phenomenon also likes to see is another high-born lady—stealing, with what a newspaper once called a few "serviceable jewels," down some sumptuous staircase for the worst of reasons. Your fashionable playwright of the Pinero-Jones-Sutro school is all for receiving erring wives at the bottom of stairs on the shirt-fronts of manly and forgiving husbands. "If ever," says one of these muscular champions, "if ever that scoundrel, the Viscount Mercredi-Jeudi-Samedi-Dimanche, lifts his eyes to you again I will thrash him within an inch of his life!" "Darling," the wife will sob, and nestle closer, her arms around his neck. But if the play is Cowardly or Arlenesque, the front door will open noiselessly, a patent-leather footstep will stealthily approach, and the minx will extend a jewelled hand behind her husband's back for Mercredi-Jeudi to kiss. This is the kind of piece whose Saturday night returns entitle it to be dubbed "great."

WHAT THE CRITIC WANTS

Here is one of the critic's, and after him the historian's, difficulties. The critic demands that plays which are not labelled fantasies shall be true to life. In other words he demands that plays shall be about real people. But the average playgoer demands that plays shall be about unreal people. The average playgoer demands that people on the stage shall be subjected to dilemmas, quandaries and concatenations of circumstance which could not by the remotest possibility happen to anybody. This cuts against the very heart of all that constitutes great drama. Aristotle —forgive me—laid it down that the object of tragedy was to purge by pity and terror, meaning that we are to feel sorry for the sufferings of the hero and heroine and be frightened by their example from doing anything which may bring a similar fate upon our own heads. One of the reasons why we hold *The Wild Duck* to be a good play is because it shows the harm that well-intentioned people may do, and demonstrates that we have no right to make a mess of other people's lives. We must be clever as well as well-intentioned, and the mess, if we must make one, should be our own mess. But the average playgoer deems *The Wild Duck* a dull play just because it is about something which might happen to anybody, and, therefore, to him. He is purged by pity and terror, and doesn't like the process—in other words he doesn't like a great play. Look at the pieces which did best in London during the year 1925. In one there is a mother and a son, as in *Hamlet*. But the son is engaged to a young lady who has been betrayed by a scoundrel. This scoundrel is the mother's lover. Now I ask the reader whether the average playgoer is nervous about *his* fiancée on any such score? Of course he isn't. Another play is about two ladies who tipple before, during and after dinner. Is the average playgoer with two sisters afraid to trust them with the decanter? Of course not. A third play is about a husband who forces his wife to dine with an entirely improper young woman. Is any playgoer who is also a husband convinced that he could, by any exercise of will, scale this topmost height of caddishness? No. These plays were successful because they dealt in situations which might conceivably happen to somebody else, but couldn't by any stretch of nervousness happen to you and me. A good criticism of these plays would be that they were amusing in spite of being untrue. Yet the canons of drama insist that a good play must be true as well as amusing. All three of the pieces alluded to above made fortunes. Whence it follows that the managers, who are not in the theatre business for their health, are tempted to put on plays which people of educated taste must condemn as merely foolish.

Let me instance two other recent plays which have had long runs, and one of which, at the time of writing, looks like being a record-breaker. In *Cobra* six foot of manhood, dressed in that kind of tweed suit which in the theatre proclaims the decent man, went to sup with a married vamp in New York's naughtiest hotel. But half-way through the meal the cool grey eyes of his sweetheart, a little shorthand-typist who had refreshed an earlier act with a cool frock of Quaker grey, flashed at the wearer of the tweeds from the depths of his sub-consciousness. So he got up from the table and left the vamp to finish her meal alone. Now what does a vamp do in the circumstances? Reason tells us that either she beckons to some unattached bachelor to finish the evening according to plan, or she goes home. What she does not do, I imagine, is to spend the night alone in the hotel, proposing to clear out at breakfast clad principally in diamonds and an opera cloak. But in the play she does this *because the dramatist is going to have the hotel burnt down that night and the poor vamp reduced to a cinder.* Whereupon the fellow in tweeds betakes himself to marriage with the typist lest another less lucky occasion reduce *his* manly body to ashes. Yet the audience did not perceive this to be nonsense—it perceived, on the contrary, that the situation and its solution were very emotional and satisfying. And the poor first-night gabies wept as bitterly as though they had attended in very sooth the actual cremating of the exquisite Miss Isabel Jeans.

HEROINES AND LUNATICS

As for *The Last of Mrs. Cheyney*, one would say that nobody outside a lunatic asylum, and few people inside one, could behave as idiotically as the heroine of this piece. Does anybody imagine that a young woman who is the head of an international gang of crooks and makes her living by pretending to be an English lady, getting herself invited to English country-houses and purloining the pearl necklaces of the week-enders—does anybody believe that such a woman, being offered £10,000 in return for a letter, would tear up the cheque and say, "I may be a pearl-thief but I am not a blackmailer?" Or that she would rather spend five years in gaol than a night in the company of a noble rip? The truth about this play is that it is a piece of obvious nonsense put together with great stage-cunning and considerable wit. And as the management has had the bright idea of enlisting Miss Gladys Cooper's beauty, Sir Gerald du Maurier's nonchalance, Mr. Ronald Squire's piquant verve and the exquisite art of Miss Ellis Jeffreys, it looks like running for five years at least. There is one aspect of play-witnessing upon which I should like to comment here, as it will be found obviously to colour the whole of this little history. This is the part which logic and truth play or should play in the theatre. When I see a woman of the gutter tearing up ten thousand pound cheques and preferring gaol to the loss of a purely hypothetical innocence I have to look round the play, so to speak, for attractions extraneous to its principal theme. It is to me as though I should be invited to look over a house of which the architect has forgotten stair-case, hall and passages. This house is uninhabitable, I should say, which is a pity, for the rooms, if you could only get to them, are charmingly decorated. But the playgoing public does not make any such distinctions. To witness the tearing-up of a cheque for ten thousand pounds is to be in at an emotional and a dramatic event, by whomsoever that cheque be torn up and for whatsoever reason. The public likes *The Last of Mrs. Cheney*, *because* of its plot, and *because* it likes to see Miss Gladys Cooper declining Sir Gerald du Maurier's invitation to be less than a perfect lady; whereas Mr. Lonsdale's cleverness consists in decorating his plot so brilliantly that you can pretend not to see its essential absurdity. An idea occurs to me here. It is that the word "play" in connection with the theatre has the same signification which we give it up in Lancashire. To the mill-hand to "play" is to be out of work, hence to be able to enjoy himself in idleness. To the average playgoer a play is something to be enjoyed without mental fatigue. Whenever, therefore, I use the word "rubbish" throughout the rest of this little book, I mean simply those works during whose concoction and absorption the intellectual faculties of author and spectator have been and are idle.

I have drawn out this tedious exposition of the plays which made most money in 1925 for the simple reason that success in the theatre is the cardinal factor in any history of the theatre. The history of the stage must always be a tale of stage-successes. And I invite the reader to turn back here to the first paragraph in this little book, where I stated that whereas the drama is an æsthetic phenomenon, the theatre is an economic proposition. In other words, there is what is known as the "commercial" theatre—by which we mean the playhouses dotting an area having Piccadilly Circus for centre and a radius of something not much over a mile—and there is the intellectual or Repertory Theatre. The history of the intellectual theatre may be—nay, indeed, must be, given the English view as to what constitutes after-dinner entertainments—a story of valiant failures and desperate semblances of something that is just not failure. Whereas, I repeat, the history of the commercial theatre must be a tale of popular successes.

But the reader must not rush to the conclusion that the popular successes of the past twenty-five years have all been rubbish. Roughly that doleful category is responsible only for some three-fourths of our money-makers. Even here we get our surprises. Not all rubbish, though it be the best streaky American, succeeds on the English stage. *The Sea-Urchin*, whose heroine was a coy young woman with a taste for travelling in a ketch full of chaste sailors, and *Pollyanna*, which was all about a feeble-minded infant of the let-a-child's-love-make-you-glad order, were almost instantaneous failures. The British public has an extraordinary knack of refusing to be stupid when you most expect it to be.

GOOD PLAYS WHICH SUCCEED

We come now to our remaining fourth of good plays—the twenty-five per cent. of really excellent pieces which the public can be bullied or goaded into seeing, or to which it takes a fancy out of some totally unfathomable caprice. I am not alluding here to the plays of Sir James Barrie, Mr. Somerset Maugham, Mr. Frederick Lonsdale, Mr. Noel Coward and Mr. Michael

Arlen—to which people in search of amusement go as automatically as they drop in to Fortnum and Mason's to buy *pâté de foie gras*. Allocating one-eighth of our successes to these playwrights there still remains one other successful eighth for which we can advance no substantial reason. Why has Mr. Eden Phillpotts' *The Farmer's Wife* run three years? It is a good comedy, but no better than a hundred others. Rumour has it that its success dated after somebody had the brilliant idea of giving a matinée for the benefit of Nonconformist country parsons. Sir Barry Jackson has told us that before the piece ran into a success he lost over two thousand pounds. Or was it six? Then there was the famous case of Mr. John Drinkwater's *Abraham Lincoln*. Hear what Mr. Nigel Playfair in his *Story of the Lyric Theatre, Hammersmith*, has to tell us of the success of this play. He says: "At its inception it was an undoubted failure. Whatever the critics might say, for some time the public would not come at all. The first matinée was played to a sum lower than that taken for any other performance at the theatre—£17. The general receipts, too, were so low as to be well below the margin set in our agreement, and it was touch-and-go whether we confessed defeat and took the play off or not." Mr. Playfair notes a slow improvement in the play's fortunes, and then follows this significant passage: "But curiously enough, our first full house was not for a performance given by Mr. Rea at all. He was called away on urgent private business, and Mr. Drinkwater was not at all pleased with the powers of his understudy. Mr. Drinkwater decided that on this occasion he would play the part himself! We bound him a copy of the script in old calf, in order that Lincoln's sudden meditative habits might not arouse suspicion; and at that performance at least Lincoln showed himself a voracious reader! The news (I will not say just how) reached the evening press; and a few hours before the curtain went up most of the evening papers had a column on the surprising news of an author suddenly playing his own lead for one night only. I don't wish in any way to detract from Mr. Drinkwater's performance, but it certainly seems odd that it was a performance *not* given by Mr. Rea which really laid the foundation stone of Mr. Rea's success in the part; and that the public, who remained unmoved by accounts of Mr. Rea's fine acting, rushed to see a performance which—for all they knew—might have been incredibly bad." So that we see quite clearly that this great piece jumped into its extraordinary popularity owing to an accident.

Does anybody imagine that Mr. Shaw's *Saint Joan* would have had its enormous success if it had been the work of some unknown Jeremiah Bloggs, of Upper Tooting? Of course not. *Saint Joan* succeeded because Mr. Shaw was popularly credited with having stood on his head for forty years and said that Shakespeare was a fool. Mr. Shaw has, of course, never said anything of the kind. What he has always said is that the intellectual content of his plays is greater than the intellectual content of Shakespeare's. And that, I venture to think, is a perfectly accurate statement. Mr. Shaw's plays have almost always been in the nature of intellectual inquiry into matters which might with equal propriety be the subject of Royal Commissions. They have contained very little humanity, and a minimum of poetry. We may even say that his drama has seldom, if ever, contained any drama. Whereas Shakespeare's plays contain all the human nature there has ever been between the ages of Pericles and Bottomley, and the finest poetry that ever sprang from the human mind. As drama they have never been equalled and will never be surpassed. But in intellectual content they are not the equal of Mr. Shaw's, any more than they can be deemed such good guides to everyday conduct as Bacon's Essays. But the reason Mr. Shaw came into his own after some forty years of struggle was because the British public thought that a man who could play the fool for so long must be a genius. They were right about the genius and wrong about the fool.

Almost it looks as though we must divide our plays not into two categories, but four. There are the indivisible goats which are the rubbish, and there are three sorts of useful sheep—the plays of excellent and fashionable Barrie, Galsworthy, Maugham and Company; the odd, inexplicable successes such as *The Farmer's Wife*, *Saint Joan*, originally produced by the devoted Lewis Casson and Sybil Thorndike in a mingled mood of exaltation and funk, and Ashley Duke's *The Man with a Load of Mischief*, in which all the theatrical prophets said there wasn't a penny; and, once more, the intellectual or Repertory Drama. In this last one includes the recent sensational successes of Ibsen and Tchehov.

It will, perhaps, be convenient to explain here why it is that now, more than ever, the story of the commercial theatre must be the story of successes. In the old days, by which I mean the 'nineties, the theatre was largely in the hands of the actor-managers. They had their faults, Heaven knows, but their severest critics have admitted that it was a mistake to fulminate so against familiar, tolerable ills and invite the public to fly to those whose horrors they could not remotely guess. At the beginning of the present century Henry Irving was still Shakespeareanly entrenched at the Lyceum; Herbert Beerbohm Tree had handsomely inaugurated a spectacular reign at his "beautiful theatre," Her Majesty's; Charles Wyndham, at the house which bears his name, was reasoning with wild young men-about-town; George Alexander was in full drawing-room blast at the St. James's; Edward Terry, at Terry's, was doing the same thing for back-parlours. At each of these theatres you knew what you were likely to get. Elderly vicars about to run up to town would say to their wives at breakfast: "Look in the *Telegraph*, my love, and see what Sir Henry or Sir Charles, or Sir George is giving us." Do our country parsons ask to-day what Mr. "Mossy" Schuncks or Mr. "Issy" Rubinstein is giving? No, for these are nonentities at the head of nameless syndicates, not here yesterday and in Carey Street or Park Lane to-morrow. In the old days there were other reputable managements besides those headed by knightly actors, and the same thing held good for the players. If you decided to go to see John Hare, or the Kendals, or Charles Hawtrey, or Lewis Waller, you knew, more or less, what sort of an evening you were in for. But say that your actor-fancy to-day lies in the direction of Leslie Faber, Edmund Gwenn or J. H. Roberts, all most admirable players; likely as not you will find them in some musical comedy, revue or dancing show. You cannot be certain to-day of finding any particular type of entertainment at any particular theatre always, of course, with certain exceptions. Thus we find the Ambassadors under Mr. H. M. Harwood, The Globe under Mr. Anthony Prinsep, the Haymarket under Mr. Frederick Harrison, the Lyceum under Messrs. W. and F. Melville, the Lyric, Hammersmith, under Mr. Nigel Playfair, the St. Martin's under Reandean Ltd.—thus we find all these theatres pursuing policies of some continuity. Daly's, the Gaiety and the Winter Garden remain faithful to musical comedy, but at the bulk of our theatres there is no telling what the playgoer may find, from revue to Tchehov.

To prove that the above is not the complaint of a disgruntled dramatic critic, I shall quote a passage from Miss Cicely Hamilton's admirable work on the *Old Vic*. Miss Hamilton says:

"The tendency of the average London playhouse has, for many years, been towards change of programme, indefinite policy and loss of distinctive character. Time was, not so long ago, when practically every theatre had its own special line—romantic, musical or farcical; but the modern West-End playhouse, as a general rule, has no settled method of attracting the public, no definite policy in the matter of plays and actors. The reason for the change is not far to seek; the modern West-End theatre passes from backer to backer and from syndicate to syndicate and is governed by no permanent authority. In the process it submits, of necessity, to chameleon-like changes of programme and policy; if its luck be out and its backers timorous it may pass in the course of a few short months (and a few short runs) from revue to tragedy, from modern farce to Shakespeare, from problem play to costume melodrama. As one attraction fails, another is tried; as one syndicate withers, another springs up in its place. So changing and passing from hand to hand, a theatre loses tradition and character; character, in any institution, is a matter of growth and permanent control—of the aims and avoidances, the likes and dislikes of those who direct its activities. A theatre controlled by a succession of syndicates, and their succession of managers, is merely a lodging-house for passing plays and the actors who present them. It stands no more chance of attaining the distinction of personality than a school would stand, if it changed all its masters once a term—or a democratic State which disposed of its rulers at every successive election."

What Miss Hamilton does not say is that these syndicates are in many cases composed of individuals whose interest in the theatre is purely financial, whose knowledge of Garrick is confined to the street, and who can scarcely put their name to a petition to be made bankrupt. If such a syndicate strike lucky all well and good; it will live to put on a piece of rubbish similar to the one which has already succeeded. If not, it melts away and disappears.

It may be instructive here to give a list of the new pieces other than musical which have run for a year, or say 350 performances, including matinées, from the beginning of 1900 to the end of 1924.

Title of Play	*Theatre*	*Date*	*No. of Perfor- mances*	*Category*
Abraham Lincoln	Lyric, H'smith	Feb. 19 1919	466	Play
Ambrose Applejohn's Adventure	Criterion	July 19 1921	455	Comedy
Bill of Divorcement, A	St Martin's	March 14 1921	401	Play
Bluebeard's Eighth Wife	Globe	August 26 1922	482	Comedy
Bull-Dog Drummond	Wyndham's	March 29 1921	429	Melodrama
Bunty Pulls the Strings	Haymarket	July 18 1911	617	S. Comedy*
By Pigeon Post	Garrick	March 30 1918	379	Play
Daddy Long-Legs	Duke of York's	May 29 1916	514	S. Comedy
Dear Brutus	Wyndham's	Oct. 17 1917	365	Fantasy
The Eyes of Youth	St. James's	Sept. 2 1918	384	Comedy
Fanny's First Play	Little	April 19 1911	624	Comedy
Farmer's Wife, The	Court	March 11 1924	†	Comedy
Flag-Lieutenant, The	Playhouse	June 16 1908	381	Naval Comedy
General Post	Haymarket	March 14 1917	532	Comedy
Glad Eye, The	Globe	Nov. 4 1912	493	Farce
Great Adventure, The	Kingsway	March 25 1913	673	Play
Green Goddess, The	St. James's	Sept. 6 1923	416	Melodrama
His House in Order	St. James's	Feb. 1 1906	430	Play
Inside the Lines	Apollo	May 23 1917	420	Anglo-Amer. Play
It Pays to Advertise	Aldwych	Feb. 1 1924	597	Farce

* Denotes sentimental comedy, or pure treacle

† Still running, 1,122nd performance, August 23, 1926

Title of Play	Theatre	Date			No. of Performances	Category
Lady Frederick	Court	Oct.	26	1907	422	Comedy
Law Divine, The	Wyndham's	August	29	1918	368	Comedy
Little Bit of Fluff, A	Criterion	Oct.	27	1915	1,241	Farce
Lord Richard in the Pantry	Criterion	Nov.	11	1919	576	Farce
Loyalties	St. Martin's	March	8	1922	407	Play
Man from Toronto, The	Royalty	May	30	1918	486	Farce
Man who Stayed at Home	Royalty	Dec.	10	1914	584	Play
Mary Rose	Haymarket	April	22	1920	399	Fantasy
Mice and Men	Lyric	Jan.	27	1902	361	S. Comedy
Milestones	Royalty	March	5	1912	607	Play
Mr. Wu	Strand	Nov.	27	1913	403	Melodrama
Monsieur Beaucaire	Comedy	Oct.	25	1902	430	Romantic Comedy
Naughty Wife, The	Playhouse	April	11	1918	598	Comedy
Nothing But the Truth	Savoy	Feb.	5	1918	578	Farce
Our Betters	Globe	Sept.	11	1923	548	Comedy
Paddy the Next Best Thing	Savoy	April	5	1920	867	S. Comedy
Peg o' my Heart	Comedy	Oct.	10	1914	710	S. Comedy
Potash and Perlmutter	Queen's	April	14	1914	665	Comedy
Purple Mask	Lyric	July	10	1918	365	Romantic Comedy
Quality Street	Vaudeville	Sept.	17	1902	459	Comedy
Raffles	Comedy	May	12	1906	351	Melodrama
Romance	Duke of York's	Oct.	6	1915	1,046	S. Comedy
Second-in-Command, The	Haymarket	Nov.	27	1900	378	S. Comedy

Title of Play	Theatre	Date	No. of Performances	Category
Secrets	Comedy	Sept. 7 1922	373	Comedy
Seven Days' Leave	Lyceum	Feb. 14 1917	711	Melodrama
Shall we join the Ladies?	St. Martin's	March 8 1922	407	Play
Skin Game, The	St. Martin's	April 21 1920	349	Play
Tilly of Bloomsbury	Apollo	July 10 1919	414	Comedy
Tons of Money	Shaftesbury	April 13 1922	937	Farce
Walls of Jericho, The	Garrick	Oct. 31 1904	423	Play
Wandering Jew, The	New	Sept. 9 1920	391	Biblical Drama
When Knights were Bold	Wyndham's	Jan. 29 1907	579	Farce
Within the Law	Haymarket	May 24 1913	451	Melodrama
You never know, y'know	Criterion	June 20 1918	327	Farce

We see from this list that, since 1900, fifty-four plays have achieved a run of six months and over. *The Farmer's Wife*, beginning as a success of esteem, continues as a triumph of determination. Barrie's name occurs four times, Arnold Bennett, John Galsworthy and Somerset Maugham are credited with two plays each and John Drinkwater, A. W. Pinero, Bernard Shaw and Alfred Sutro with one play each. The other authors are hardly likely to come up for consideration in any history of the stage. Note that *Saint Joan*, moving from theatre to theatre, is still alive after something like two years, and that there is always Charles Macdona's company of players whose repertory is Shaw, the whole Shaw and nothing but Shaw. Yet it is surely significant that this list should not contain the names of Henry Arthur Jones, Haddon Chambers, Hubert Henry Davies, Granville Barker, St. John Hankin, John Masefield, Stanley Houghton and Elizabeth Baker. Of the crowd of younger intellectuals there is, of course, no example.

Analysed, the list given above will be found to show twelve serious plays as against forty-two light comedies and farces. Yet in the same period no fewer than eighty-five musical comedies and revues had runs of six months and over. Truly it looks as if Professor Morley was right when he said in 1858:

"There must be a deeper earnestness than plays can demand, in whatever serious thing Englishmen are to look at without exercise of that sense of the humorous which is part of their life; so natural a part that every man is in every grade of society regarded as a bore who wants it; and the very phrase with thousands even among our educated men for not finding a thing acceptable is 'seeing no fun' in it."

WHY PLAYS MUST PAY

Now it may be said that this matter of a six months' run is not a fair test for drama. It isn't. But it is an admirable test for the theatre which, as we have already laid down, is an entirely different pair of shoes. In the old days an actor-manager who held his theatre on a long lease at reasonable price, and moreover had his accumulations of scenery and his regular company of actors—such a manager could afford to put on a non-rubbishy, non-musical piece and "nurse" it into a success.

The astute manager will make a distinction between the intelligent piece, such for example as Pinero's *His House in Order* which, from the word "go," had all the elements of a popular success, and the intellectual masterpiece, as an example of which one might cite Granville Barker's *The Voysey Inheritance*. It has been proved over and over again that the London audience for any intellectual play is forty thousand and no more. Now if these forty thousand can be got into the theatre in six weeks the play will, financially speaking, just about pay its way. If this maximum audience takes twelve weeks to make up its mind, then the venture will incur a loss. It may be interesting to note what Mr. Shaw has to say on this point. He is talking of the production, in 1894, of *Arms and the Man* by the Independent Theatre.

"This play ran from the 21st of April to the 7th July. To witness it the public paid £1,777 5*s*. 6*d*., an average of £23 2*s*. 5*d*. per representation (including nine matinées). A publisher receiving £1,700 for a book would have made a satisfactory profit; experts in theatrical management will contemplate that figure with a grim smile. This, however, need not altogether discourage speculators in twentieth century drama. If the people who were willing to pay £1,700 to see the play had all come within a fortnight instead of straggling in during twelve weeks—and such people can easily be trained to understand this necessity—the result would have been financially satisfactory to the management and at least flattering to the author."

But Mr. Shaw is wrong in saying that the intelligentsia can be trained. They can't, being, in this particular, less wise than the regular first-nighter who knows that the only night which any play can be sure of is its first. Hundreds of alleged intelligent playgoers try to book seats at plays whose runs finished a month ago. The English public, intellectual or stupid, hardly knows that a good piece is on until it is nearly dead of inanition, and generally wants to see it only when it has been taken off, thus proving the English a great nation for hurrying up the oxygen after the patient has been laid out.

We have seen that the actor-manager could have his little flutter in intelligent, as distinct from intellectual drama, without risking his life's savings. If A's play failed he lost £1,000 or so and put on B's. But the actor-manager is virtually extinct, and it is here that we come up against the syndicate which has no interest in the theatre other than the financial, and that even more sinister individual, the sweep who rents a theatre not for the purpose of producing plays but in order to let that theatre to some other sweep at a profit-rental. The reader may say that it is of no interest to the public who owns the theatres, and that we, as playgoers, are concerned only with the pieces which we pay our money to see. But the whole point is that the quality and variety of the plays which the public has the opportunity of seeing are affected, not by the identity of the person who originally owns the theatre, but by the number of hands through which the sub-leases pass before we arrive at the presenter of the piece. Because, you see, each person through whose hands the lease passes takes a profit out of it. What happens is that Mr. Jones who owns the theatre—and by owning it I mean pays a first rent of say £100 per week—sublets it to Mr. Smith at, say, £200 per week. Mr. Smith sublets it again to Mr. Brown at £275 per week, Mr. Brown sublets it to Mr. Robinson at £350, Mr. Robinson sublets it to Mr. Jenkins at £400, and Mr. Jenkins finally lets it to somebody, who actually wants to produce a play, at £450. Now it should be realised that Smith, Brown, Robinson and Jenkins are not concerned with the drama or with play-producing, the interest of each of them being entirely confined to the amount of money he can make by letting the theatre out to his successor. What, then, happens? Now let us go back to the actor-manager. The actor-manager's rent was low, his scenery could often be altered and adapted from one play to another, the salaries of himself and his wife were virtually non-existent owing to their being content to come in on the profits. It is to be imagined, therefore, that he could produce many plays at a cost of not more than £700 or £800 per week. But even plays which are reckoned dead failures draw to-day as much as £400 a week into the box office, and you may put a moderate or commencing success at £600 a week. You can see, therefore, that in the old days many plays which were doubtful did not cost the actor-manager more than £200 per week to nurse. At the end of five weeks' nursing he would not have lost more than £1,000. Now, with the enormously increased rent of theatres and the large salaries drawn by leading actors, it is safe to say that few plays are put on at a West-End theatre under £1,400 per week. If the play takes £400 the theatre loses £1,000 a week; if it takes £600 it loses £800 per week and so on. Some London play-producing firms are content to lose thousands of pounds on a production in London so that the piece may be afterwards sent into the provinces stamped with the name of a London theatre and the words "West-End Success," in the hope of getting back in the country what has been lost in town and something more on top. But many plays are being written which, in so far as they are serious contributions to the drama, have not got the spurious hall-mark stamped all over them. And, therefore, there is no inducement to anybody to produce them at all.

AND PAY AT ONCE

I should like to make two observations here. My first is that people who take what I call an intelligent interest in the Theatre never have any money. My second is that the people who have money never take an intelligent interest in the Theatre. The most the wealthy will do is to flock to fashionable play-houses and rail at the bad plays; it never enters their heads to attend unfashionable theatres and praise the good plays. Will anyone maintain that our millionaires flock to the Old Vic? Or deny that their shirt fronts gleam and glisten for the bedazzlement of the beauty-chorus of such light entertainments as *Spank Me*, or *Shingle and Bob?* "'Ave a bit of common!" as we say in Lancashire. The matter is easily put to the test. Approach a millionaire, tell him that you have got a play for which you want him to put up the money. "What sort of play?" he will ask. "A light comedy," you say. "Good!" he replies, "I suppose three thousand will see you through." You begin to elaborate. "A light farcical comedy." "Splendid!" he chuckles, "I'll put up five thousand for that." "An imbecile light farcical comedy," you continue, "with a part for Miss Pepsicum Tiddleywinks." "Better and better," he chortles, "make it ten thousand." But take the other side of the picture. Suppose you tell your millionaire that you have got a good play, true to life, written with fine observation and in nervous English, without a shade of nastiness and essentially noble—propose that and you will then have before you an object lesson in natural history.

Humanity may or may not be descended from the ape, but it cannot be doubted that your theatrical millionaire is first cousin to the hedgehog. Poke your hedgehog with a walking-stick and you know what happens. Shove such a proposition as I have mentioned at your theatrical millionaire and he will roll up into a bundle of spiky, indignant horror. "Not an earthly," he will snarl, "such a play would not draw tuppence! Get out!"

But sometimes it happens that a man who takes an intelligent interest in the Theatre has a little money. Let us take the case of three such men. A has £1,000, B has £2,000, and C has £5,000. Let us suppose that each is going to back a play of which neither the scenery nor the dressing is elaborate. However simple the production, you may reckon that after the producer's fee is paid, any piece, however economically put on, will have cost round about £500. I am not talking of a Repertory Company, where pieces are produced every week, but of an isolated production. That £500 has to all intents and purposes gone west, and it is the same for our three men, A, B and C. Now take the running expenses. With theatre rents at £400 a week you may put down £800 a week as a very low estimate.

This includes the salaries of the company, and all expenses back and front of the house, lighting, advertising, etc., etc. Suppose now that you only take £300 a week, a figure sufficiently flattering in the case of a really first-class intellectual play. What has happened at the end of the first week? Take A's case first; he has spent £800 during the week, and taken £300 for seats. Loss on the week £500. But he has already sunk £500 of his capital. Add £500 to £500 and the result is £1,000. Because, however topsy-turvey the theatrical world is in other respects, two and two still continue to make four. It is the inability to recognise this fact which has led to so many failures in theatrical ventures. Then what has our £1,000 man to do? He has lost his money and, therefore, must close down at once. Now take B. B's case is a little better. He has lost £1,000 out of his £2,000, but he has enough money left to run for two more weeks at a loss of £500 a week, or three more weeks at a loss of £330. But at the end of three weeks his £2,000 will be exhausted, and the play will be over. Now take C. His case is altogether different. After the first week when he, like the others, has lost his £1,000, he has still £4,000 left, on which, provided he has the pluck, he can afford to stick it for yet another eight weeks at a loss of £500 a week. Now, the reader may ask why should one throw good money after bad? And the answer is: "One should never throw good money after bad. But be quite sure that the money *is* bad." Very few plays, except perfectly proper musical comedy, and perfectly improper prose comedies, and the admirable farces sponsored by Messrs. Tom Walls and Leslie Henson, jump into popularity straight away. It is no secret that that excellent piece, *White Cargo*, ran for a considerable time to very considerable losses. The playgoer may ask: "What has this got to do with me?" and I answer: "Everything!"

Frankly, at this point I would make an appeal to people who take their play-going seriously and are anxious that good plays should not be allowed to perish on our stage. I am no opponent of the lighter form of entertainment, and consider an evening at the music hall with such artists as May Henderson or Will Fyffe in the bill to be almost the apex of human felicity on this earth. Fortunately life has many such summits. But the theatre has its peak of lonely grandeur which the great play inhabits, and this is where the class of playgoer to whom

I now appeal comes in. "If you know of a better 'ole, go to it," said Old Bill, and I say, "If you hear of a good play go to it, and go *at once.*" It makes a world of difference whether you go now or in three weeks' time. He goes to the theatre twice who goes quickly.

But the point I want to make is that the financiers who are the bane of the modern drama, though possibly a boon to custumiers, perruquiers, scenic-artists and scene-shifters, have got too much money. They have no interest in the drama and, therefore, they look round for the largest profits. A piece which should hold the boards for less than six months does not interest them. A three months' run, which in the days of the actor-manager meant a very fair success and a quite profitable one, will not to-day "see its own back." In other words the initial cost of production will have been barely recovered. A six months' run represents, to immoderate men, only a very moderate success. Financiers are not fools, and they are certainly clever enough to have found out what my list of plays with long runs proves—and this was the reason for giving it—that of all entertainments which have made money in London the musical and the frivolous have formed an overwhelming proportion. This being demonstrated, the fiat of the syndicates has gone forth: *No money for serious drama: bags of it for tosh.*

BACK TO THE WALL

The drama of to-day, then, has to make headway against the syndicating managers, against the degeneration in taste occasioned by the war, against the inventions of wireless and the cinema, against the craze for dancing, against the improved railway facilities which enable the business man to live and maintain his family thirty miles from town, against the taste for motoring and the advent of the motor-bike.

It might be held that the wise historian is he who refuses to meddle with what may be called the politics of the theatre. But all theories can be carried too far, including this one. A small anecdote comes to my mind here. I remember when I was a very young man trying to explain Tolstoy's doctrine of submission and non-interference to a grave and distinguished author who was old enough to be twice my father. "Tolstoy lays it down," I said, and you will please remember that I was a very young man indeed, "Tolstoy lays it down that if you find another man hitting your wife over the head with a chopper and cutting the children up into mincemeat you must let him do it and not interfere." "Ah!" said my friend reflectively, stroking his beard. After a pause he added: "Do you think it would be permitted to walk away?"

Well, dear readers, I am sure that nobody who would write of the English theatre in the last twenty-five years can afford to walk away from its economic side. Let me say here that whether the theatre managers make money or lose it has never been any business of the dramatic critic. The box office side of the theatre has nothing, never has had anything, and never can have anything to do with dramatic criticism. The absence of any financial or box office side, or the case of no money coming in, is the concern of the critic only when the play fails because it is too good. Then, and then only, is he justified in attempting a rescue. But if some financial magnate likes to risk £10,000 in putting on an indifferent musical comedy with a wretched book and feeble music, silly scenery and stupid acting, it is nobody's concern except his own if his venture fails. He has not put the thing on for the sake of art or to amuse the public. He has put it on to amuse himself by getting money out of the public, and the public has refused to be gulled. Such a manager is less deserving of sympathy than the store-keeper who has bought 20,000 umbrellas in anticipation of the English summer, and has been disappointed.

Why should playgoers judge the play by the tally of other playgoers? Nobody argues that the number of people who pass the turnstiles of the National Gallery affects the quality of Titian or Van Dyck, and not even the most rabid materialist pretends that the number of enthusiasts at the Oval on a bank-holiday determines the size of Hobbs's score. The box office side of the theatre has as little to do with the playgoer as with the critic.

NOT A FREE ART

But the historian is in a different case from either. He must not write of the theatre as though it were an art-form magnoperating in the void. He must not attempt to judge it as he would a free art trying to express itself in the best possible way and with everybody anxious to help. That may be the drama, but it is not the theatre. The theatre is just as good as its enemies will allow it to be, and no better. It has to fight the imbecility of financial speculators who believe that the public will pay to see nothing except rubbish, and the apathy of the serious playgoer who too often lends colour to the managerial contention.

But here we come upon what at first sight would appear to be an extraordinary feature of the situation. This feature is that whereas the theatre in England is dying, the drama was never healthier. Repertory theatres are springing up all over the country, thousands of playgoers are meeting in the smaller towns and even in the villages to read and discuss plays. A greater number of intellectual plays has been produced in London in the last two years than at any previous time, and on the whole these plays have either not lost money, or lost very little. Though the theatre of Shaftesbury Avenue may be numb and dead, all around the tiny area of morbidity the land is a-swarm with life. The phenomenon is not a new one. The advent of the novel killed the business of writing verses for a living, but it did not destroy poetry. The advent of the speculative manager has killed the theatre in fashionable London—with the exception of such plays as have the good fortune to deal with harlotry in some form or another—but it has not in any way affected the drama. The drama is as much alive to-day in this country as it ever was, and at the present moment there is, if I may so express myself, a hell of a kick in it. It now becomes my business to describe the fall of the theatre and the rise of the drama during the last twenty-five years.

EARLY HISTORY

It may be as well to consider for a little what the position of the English stage was prior to the great outburst of dramatic activity which began just before the close of the Victorian era. The nineteenth century had been a period largely made up of decay and disappointment. Its early years saw the retirement of Mrs. Siddons and John Philip Kemble, with whom the grand style of acting definitely passed away. Great actors of other styles abounded, but there was an almost complete lack of good playwrights to support even good second-rate players. Sheridan Knowles and Bulwer-Lytton succeeded plentifully in falling between two stools—the bombastic throne to which their genius was unequal and the domestic chair which they had not common sense enough to fill. But then the domestic chair was as yet hardly in evidence. Knowles died in 1862, which must be my excuse for saying no more about him, and Lytton eleven years later. It was in 1838 and the two following years that Bulwer wrote the three works which were his masterpieces—*The Lady of Lyons*, *Richelieu* and *Money*. It is always quaintly said of these plays that they have kept the stage ever since. What this means I do not know. There is no living actor or actress who could cope with the rodomontade of Pauline and her lover, and if there were, modern taste would not put up with them. I know of no performances in recent years with the exception of "command" performances, or performances for charity. Professor Morley has an admirable description of the state of the English stage during the years which preceded the coming of Robertson, and I imagine that a great deal that he wrote then would hold good even in our own time. "There is," says Morley, "a large half-intelligent population that by bold puffing can be got into a theatre. It numbers golden lads and lassies as well as chimney-sweeps. The population is, indeed, so large that it takes many nights to pass it through a theatre, each night's theatre-full being as a bucket-full dipped out of a big stagnant pond. Any manager may, if he will, set his face against intelligent opinion, and, falling back upon the half-intelligent, go the right way to that pond, bale patiently and send nearly the whole of it through his house . . . Against the condemnation of his piece by every educated man he can set the advertisement that Duchesses and Viscounts have been to see it, and that it is being acted for its millionth night." All of which applies very accurately to present day conditions. The whole of theatrical history in the 'fifties and 'sixties is the history of the inferior works of the French stage; nearly all English plays of the period are translations or adaptations from what the Professor so felicitously calls *Pomme Pourrie* by MM. Péché and Bonbon.

Enfin Robertson vint. Born in 1829 he was thirty-five years old when he committed the crime known as *David Garrick*, for which he was sentenced to be acted by amateurs for ever. The following year saw *Society* produced at, and Society flocking to, the Prince of Wales Theatre. This little house in Tottenham Street was under the management of Marie Wilton, afterwards Mrs., and later Lady Bancroft. *Ours* was produced in 1866, *Caste* in 1867, *Play* in 1868, *School* in 1869, *M.P.* in 1870. Of these *Caste* still "holds the stage," in the sense that performances are given from time to time for money and not out of mere curiosity. Those who are interested may like to note that in the year in which *Caste* was produced, Browning published *The Ring and the Book*, Dickens was at work upon his last novel, and William Morris was writing the first volumes of *The Earthly Paradise*.

For some time yet it seemed as though these plays of Robertson's were to be the only realistic stones cast into the pool of balderdash. The success of H. J. Byron's *Our Boys*, which ran at the Vaudeville Theatre from January, 1875, till April, 1879, plunged the stage into a flood of Byronism of the worst sort. As an actor Byron had neither originality nor charm; as a playwright he was hardly more than a punster.

Then within three years appeared three plays by three writers, two of whom were to have an immense influence on the English commercial theatre as distinct from the theatre of ideas. Only, of course, one must always credit our commercial theatre with sufficient gumption to take up with her less fashionable sister for such period as there is any money in her. That is why the "problem plays" of Arthur Wing Pinero and Henry Arthur Jones were so successful. English society, having heard vaguely of Ibsen's problematic heroes and heroines, was all agog to have expounded to it problems of its own people. Pinero and Jones obliged accordingly with theses suited to Mayfair's mood, tacking on to them solutions whose essential falsity made them extremely palatable to the modish playgoer. Vanity was tickled at being asked to think in the theatre without any loss of complacency resulting from that thought. In the meantime we must go back to our three little plays—Pinero's *Two Hundred a Year*, which appeared in 1877, Jones's *Only Round the Corner*, produced in 1878, and Sydney Grundy's *The Snowball*, staged in 1879.

Grundy is easily disposed of. He wrote nothing that will live because he never wrote anything that was alive. *A Pair of Spectacles* (1890) was sentimental melodrama freely adapted from *Les Petits Oiseaux* of Labiche and Delacour; *A Fool's Paradise* (1892) was a pure domestic tragedy; *Sowing the Wind* (1893) had to do with illegitimate children;. and *A Bunch of Violets* (1894), for which the author went to Octave Feuillet, was a "melodramatic domestic problem drama." In the last two plays Grundy was certainly tarred, as Clement Scott would have said, with the Ibsen brush. But this playwright had no mind, and one feels that he chose to deal in pitch only because defilement was *à la mode*.

THE PROBLEM PLAY

Perhaps the English theatre can give no more significant proof of growth than the general use in the 'nineties of the phrase, "the problem play." To-day we take it for granted that a piece shall state some problem in life, conduct or manners. The problem is not necessarily sexual, and we do not spend our evenings debating whether the children of syphilitic parents should take one another in marriage. Wasserman has settled that question. To-day we ask whether there is a spirit-land, and whether in the next world a mother who died when her son was a babe will be glad to welcome a strapping middle-aged man with quarter-deck manners (*Mary Rose*). Or whether mothers should encourage their sons to dope

(*The Vortex*). Or whether the French had not plentiful reason to thank the English for ridding them of their turbulent priestess (*Saint Joan*). Before the 'nineties it had never entered the heads of playgoers that they might be called upon to use them, and when they were so called upon they grew portentous and talked of "problems"; to-day we presume that the play is for beings with power of ratiocination unless the words "light" or "farcical" comedy warn us to the contrary. I feel sure that charming and clever Messrs. Tom Walls and Leslie Henson will not mind my saying that to-day the answer to the riddle: "When is a play not a problem play?" is "When it's at the Aldwych Theatre."

The problem-play, so called, was first heralded into the commercial theatre in England by Pinero's *The Second Mrs. Tanqueray* (1893) and continued in vogue with Jones's *Michael and his Lost Angel* (1896). But there was an enormous amount of playwriting in this country between the last flicker of Byron's punning and the first flicker of the intellectual drama. There was Oscar Wilde, first-rate wit and man of the theatre, second-rate poet and tenth-rate everything else. As a dramatist Wilde was like an architect who should be so highly absorbed in his ornamentations that he forgot his constructions; there is no play of his which would not have fallen down if he had not relied upon some older builder to put its bricks together for him. His plots are hoary with the dexterity of previous generations. "This play," wrote C. E. Montague, of *An Ideal Husband*, "shows how indolently a man of comic genius may write a comedy and yet not fail. Plot, incident, and in outline, characters are half-invented, half-cribbed, as lazily or hurriedly as anything in Shakespeare or Molière, the arch-cribbers. As mainspring to a play the blackmailing lady who keeps whole catacombs of dark pasts, steals jewels freely, and is received at embassies may, indeed, be junior to the everlasting hills—it depends on the age of the hills—but the world of stormed barns and penny gaffs has no older inhabitants." The same critic goes on to discuss at length the peculiar quality of Wilde's wit:

"But the play of mind of Wilde's Londoners of quality is that of English men and women whom a very witty Frenchman or Irishman is coaching, prompting, briefing, and at the same time watching, delicately mocking. Behind the immediate gaiety and irony of their talk you feel a reserve of irony not given to them but playing upon them, and, through them, on their audience; it comes out in the more obvious epigrams, thrown like little bombs as if to match with their shouted emphasis some assumed dullness and literalness in the hearer's mind; and again it comes out in the reticent gravity with which Chiltern, the public man, the phrasing dullard, is presented, as if Wilde half thought that the public might take him seriously, and, for mischief's sake, would not give them the hint not to do so. The thing is so drenched in comedy that it cannot but keep an audience laughing, but with the laughter there goes some perplexity, and, we fancy, an uneasy sense of something alien to the spectator's blood and of a general blurring of the confines of lawful fun and levity."

This admirable criticism holds the key of the whole virtue of Wilde—his sense of the importance of not being in earnest. The "lawful confines" may be blurred, but they are blurred wilfully; the tongue must be in the cheek or its owner yawned.

Then there was Haddon Chambers, a popular playwright, who achieved a number of comedies of sentiment and satire of which the best known is *The Idler* (1891) and the best written *The Tyranny of Tears* (1899). This playwright accomplished the bulk of his work before 1900, only four plays coming from his pen between that date and 1921, when he died.

1893 AND 1900

The reader may have gathered that what I am trying to do here is to present two pictures of the English stage—one prior to 1893, the year when drama, taking a dive in Norwegian waters, suffered a permanent sea-change, and as it was in 1900, the year when this little survey is supposed to begin. It is a curious thing, incidentally, that Bancroft, who was an indifferent actor, should have exerted through Robertson an enormous influence on the English drama, and that Irving, an actor of genius, the successor to Kean, Kemble and Macready, and a figure of paramount importance on the English stage throughout the 'eighties and 'nineties, should have had no influence at all. As far as English playwriting is concerned, Irving might as well never have existed.

Prior to 1893 Pinero had written fifteen plays which to-day are only names and hardly that. In 1885 he inaugurated with *The Magistrate* that series of brilliant farces which are equal to the best of Labiche, bringing the series to an end in 1893 with *The Amazons*. These little pieces show this playwright as a first-class man of the theatre and a *vaudevilliste* of genius. During this period Henry Arthur Jones was busy collaborating with Henry Herman in *The Silver King* (1886) and *Chatterton* (1884) and with Wilson Barrett in *Hoodman Blind* (1885) and *The Lord Harry* (1886). The titles of other plays of his round about this time are sufficiently expressive —*The Noble Vagabond*, *Hard Hit*, *Heart of Hearts*, etc. And one believes that it is in *Michael and his Lost Angel* that the author is first found sensitive to the new wind blowing through English drama.

It is time now to mention the biggest man in the English, and the second biggest man in the world-theatre since Shakespeare. George Bernard Shaw, born at Dublin in 1856, began life in a land-agent's office. But his interest in two subjects so apparently disparate as music and political science soon drove him from a country in which there was neither to one overflowing with concert-mongers and carpet-baggers. In this happy land Shaw at once blazed forth as a literary hack of the first magnitude, writing coruscating stuff for dear life and a pittance. He became art critic to the *World* and *Truth*, musical critic to the *Star* and the *World*, and in the early 'nineties dramatic critic to the *Saturday Review*, revealing in each of these posts an uncanny knack of knowing the bottom of his subject from sonatas to sewage. But sewage, the reader may object, does not come into dramatic criticism. It didn't before Shaw. Now this great critic, possessing, as Mr. Chesterton has pointed out, all the calm, dispassionate reasoning quality of the Irishman, soon came to see that it was useless to appeal to the absence of logic in the emotional Englishman. What was he to do with a race which worshipped Shakespeare and avoided seeing him acted, translated Darwin's "Some monkeys have no tails" into "All men have had tails," and made a god of Dan Leno? Why, simply stand on his head, and in manner and phrase of utmost flippancy, parade the most devout of his philosophy. The English will always lend ear to a buffoon even when he is shamming, and Shaw saw to it that no man ever shammed harder. Shakespeare he declared to be a master-musician and a duffer at political science, whereby the English understood him to say that though Shakespeare was a first-class sociologist, he couldn't write plays. What Shaw said and meant was that though Shakespeare's dramas were better than those of any other man, as economic tracts for the times they were rubbish; whereas his, Shaw's, plays were magnificent gospels and those who didn't consider them good plays otherwise needn't. And the English, given the choice between liking a good new thing and lumping it, lumped it. They lumped it for a considerable period, until such time, in fact, as the rest of the educated world including even America had accepted Shaw as a dramatist of the first class. Fashionable London went on cold-shouldering this writer long after the provinces had accepted him, until it perceived at last that to be the laughing-stock of the polite world was no longer *chic*. It is not that Shaw made no efforts to conciliate popular taste. He did make such efforts, notably in *You Never Can Tell*, where he deliberately set out to study "the popular preference for fun, fashionable dresses, a little music, and even an exhibition of eating and drinking by people with an expensive air, attended by an, if possible, comic waiter."

The difficulty about the Shaw plays is that they are well known to be the work of an intellectual, and that in the early 'nineties intellect was not the general taste. (Neither is it in 1926. See the instantaneous failure of *The Prisoners of War*.) And the coteries and the Sunday night societies were not yet. But they were just beginning, and the name which must now be written is the honoured one of J. T. Grein. In 1891 Grein, with the help of a few associates, founded The Independent Theatre, which gave performances of Shaw's *Widowers' Houses*, Zola's *Thérèse Raquin* and Ibsen's *Ghosts*. In the preface to a volume of Grein's dramatic criticism printed in 1921 the reader will find the following letter from Shaw:

"It is now very close on thirty years since you madly began an apparently hopeless attempt to bring the English theatre into some sort of relation with contemporary culture. Matthew Arnold had suggested that step; but nobody in the theatre took the slightest notice of him, because nobody in the theatre knew of the existence of such a person as Matthew Arnold. . . . When you first desperately stuck an advertisement into the papers to say that an unheard-of enterprise called the Independent Theatre would, on a certain Sunday night and Monday afternoon, perform an unheard-of play . . . when the papers thereon declared that the manager of the theatre ought to be prosecuted for keeping a disorderly house, and that you and the foreign blackguard named Ibsen, who was your accomplice, should be deported as obvious undesirables, you made a hole in the dyke; and the weight of the flood outside did the rest. When you declared that you would bring to light treasures of unacted English drama grossly suppressed by the managers of that day, you found that there was not any unacted English drama except two acts of an unfinished play (begun and laid aside eight years before) by me; but it was the existence of the Independent Theatre that made me finish that play. . . . Everything followed from that: the production of *Arms and the Man*, Miss Horniman's establishment of Repertory Theatres in Dublin and Manchester, the Stage Society, Granville Barker's tentative matinées of *Candida* at the Court Theatre, the full-blown management of Vedrenne and Barker, Edie Craig's Pioneers, and the final relegation of the nineteenth century London theatre to the dust-bin by Barrie."

"THE SECOND MRS. TANQUERAY"

Two years after the founding of the Independent Theatre, Pinero produced *The Second*

Mrs. Tanqueray, which proved none of the things it set out to prove, and demonstrated a lot that the author never intended—that marriage with an *exalté* like Aubrey Tanqueray is an infliction beyond the endurance of any woman of spirit, respectable or otherwise, that life in an English country house must inevitably lead to suicide, and that "under a queer fantastic light at night or in the glare of the morning, that horrid, irresistible truth that physical repulsion forces on men and women" will come to Tanqueray, and he will realise that Paula has "gone off" in the same way as, and no differently from, Mrs. Cortelyon or any other decent woman. As a warning to adventuresses the play was a failure—that Cyprian would indeed be lacking in dash who boggled at the million-to-one chance of a former protector falling in love with his successor's daughter. As a tragedy it failed also—there being nothing particularly tragic or even impolite about Ardale's union with Ellean. But Pinero is such a master of the stage in all things not of the first importance that the play, in conjunction with the great talent of Mrs. Patrick Campbell, had an immense success. The hypercritical may say that Pinero, having taken the trouble to learn

Ibsen's language, was in this piece heard to speak it indifferently, but the fact remains that *The Second Mrs. Tanqueray* is a great stage-play which, in spite and perhaps because of its evasions, has always had the power to move an audience so long as there has been an actress with the power to play Paula. But suppose that flamboyant lady had chosen to go off again with Ardale and leave Aubrey and Ellean to an interchange of priggish consolation? Or that Paula had discovered Tanqueray to be the father not of a grown-up daughter, but of a grown-up son to whom she "was not a stranger"? Or simply that she had decided that she could not "stick" respectability whether Ardale turned up or not, and had taken the next train back to Claridge's or whatever hotel was in vogue in 1893? Would the audience have embraced a living woman as they embraced one who committed suicide for no discoverable reason? The answer is in the negative. A real live Paula would have been immoral, one who commits suicide needed no white-washing.

In *Michael and his Lost Angel*, Henry Arthur Jones put another question and, like his confrère, ran away from the answer. Of this piece Shaw remarked: "As to the first two acts, I ask nothing better; but at the beginning of the third comes the parting of our ways; and I can point out the exact place where the roads fork. In the first act, Michael, a clergyman, compels a girl who has committed what he believes to be a deadly sin, to confess it publicly in church. In the second act he commits that sin himself. At the beginning of the third act he meets the lady who has been his accomplice; and the following words pass between them:

"Audrie: You're sorry?

"Michael: No. And you?

"Audrie: No.

"Now, after this, what does the clergyman do? Without giving another thought to the all-significant fact that he is not sorry—that at the very point where, if his code and creed were valid, his conscience would be aching with remorse, he is not only impenitent, but positively glad, he proceeds to act as if he really were penitent, and not only puts on a hair shirt, but actually makes a confession to his congregation in the false character of a contrite sinner, and goes out from among them with bowed head to exile and disgrace, only waiting in the neighbourhood until the church is empty to steal back and privily contradict his pious imposture by picking up and hiding a flower which the woman has thrown on the steps of the altar."

TOSH, BUT GOOD TOSH

In other words the solution to the situation was pure tosh. But there is this to be said for the playwright—that he did at least have the courage to state his situation, the date being 1896. In the theatre the play obtained a very fair amount of success. For the plays of Pinero and Jones, whatever else they may not be, are always exciting after the manner of those newspapers which never fail to make the reader believe that something of importance happened yesterday. The years between 1893 and 1900 are noteworthy principally for the increasing prowess of these two playwrights. During this time Pinero wrote *The Notorious Mrs. Ebbsmith*, *The Benefit of the Doubt*, *The Princess and the Butterfly*, *Trelawney of the Wells*, and *The Gay Lord Quex*, while Jones's principal contribution was that brilliant comedy *The Liars*. Both these playwrights, it cannot be too strongly insisted, are masters of the theatre. Both show an immense advance in technique and subject-matter upon the theatre of Robertson, Boucicault, Taylor and Grundy. In their hands the intellectual gap between the English novel and the English drama was lessened from a hundred years to fifty.

THE RENAISSANCE

The years between the beginning of the century and the beginning of the war mark a period of the greatest dramatic energy in this country since the Elizabethans. The Stage Society began the good work with a performance, on November 20th, 1899, of Shaw's *You Never Can Tell.* But there can be no doubt that the great spur to the movement was the Vedrenne-Barker venture at the Court Theatre between 1904 and 1907. The spur was also the occasion. For dramatic energy must find an outlet elsewhere than between the covers of a book—it needs a playhouse, actors and an audience. Mr. Vedrenne and Mr. Granville Barker provided all three. In this short space of time they produced thirty-two plays by the most distinguished authors of the day. The full list of plays and authors is as follows:

Play	*Author*	*Performances*
Man and Superman	Bernard Shaw	176
You Never Can Tell	,, ,,	149
John Bull's Other Island	,, ,,	121
Capt. Brassbound's Conversion	,, ,,	89
Major Barbara	,, ,,	52
The Doctor's Dilemma	,, ,,	50
Prunella	Housman and Barker	48
The Voysey Inheritance	Granville Barker	34
Candida	Bernard Shaw	31
The Silver Box	John Galsworthy	29
Votes for Women	Elizabeth Robins	23
The Electra	Euripides	20
The Hippolytus	,,	20
The Return of the Prodigal	St. John Hankin	19
The Thieves' Comedy	Gerhart Hauptmann	9
The Pot of Broth	W. B. Yeats	9
In the Hospital	A. Schnitzler	9
How he Lied to her Husband	Bernard Shaw	9
The Trojan Women	Euripides	8
The Charity that Began at Home	St. John Hankin	8
The Reformer	Cyril Harcourt	8
The Campden Wonder	John Masefield	8
The Philanderer	Bernard Shaw	8
Don Juan in Hell	,, ,,	8
The Man of Destiny	,, ,,	8
Hedda Gabler	Henrik Ibsen	7
Aglavaine and Selysette	M. Maeterlinck	6
The Wild Duck	Henrik Ibsen	6
Pan and the Young Shepherd	Maurice Hewlett	6
The Youngest of the Angels	,, ,,	6
A Question of Age	R. V. Harcourt	2
The Convict on the Hearth	F. Fenn.	2
		988

The casts of these performances included such distinguished players as:

Kate Rorke	Granville Barker
Sydney Fairbrother	Norman McKinnel
Edyth Olive	Alfred Brydone
Rosina Filippi	Ben Webster
Agnes Thomas	A. E. George
Ellen O'Malley	Louis Calvert
Florence Farr	J. L. Shine
Ada Ferrar	Wilfred Shine
Marie Brema	Nigel Playfair
Edith-Wynne-Mathison	Graham Browne
Gertrude Kingston	A. E. George
Lillah McCarthy	C. V. France
Mrs. Theodore Wright	Athole Stewart
Tita Brand	John Deverell
Sarah Brooke	Lewis Casson
Dorothy Minto	C. M. Hallard
Henrietta Watson	J. D. Beveridge
Clare Greet	Norman Page
Madge McIntosh	Edmund Gwenn
Fanny Brough	James Hearn
Mabel Hackney	Dennis Eadie
Mary Brough	A. G. Poulton
Ellen Terry	Hubert Harben
Francis Ivor	J. H. Barnes
Irene Rooke	Scott Buist

Grace Lane
Eva Moore
Carlotta Addison
Penlope Wheeler
Mrs. Patrick Campbell
Evelyn Weeden
Adela Measor
Miss Fortescue
Irene Vanbrugh

Matheson Lang
O. B. Clarence
Dawson Milward
Harcourt Williams
Frederick Kerr
Henry Ainley
Michael Sherbrooke
William Haviland
William Poel
Allan Aynesworth
Sydney Brough
H. R. Hignett
Eric Lewis
Trevor Lowe
Laurence Irving
Edmund Gurney
Aubrey Smith
Holman Clark
A. E. Mathews
Robert Loraine
Dion Boucicault

Each of these performances was a new conquest over dullness on the English stage. How good for the playgoer and how good, too, for the player! The Vedrenne-Barker venture made fashionable what Shaw, in the preface to his volume entitled *Pleasant Plays* called the public-spirited manager, of whom the definition is that he keeps as close as he can to the highest marketable limit of quality, and constantly feels for an extension of that limit through the advance of popular culture. Such a manager will give his customers what they want and understand, "or even enough of it to induce them to swallow at the same time a great deal that they neither want nor understand."

The intellectual movement was given an enormous fillip when it received as a recruit the always esteemed and regretted Charles Frohman, who, in January, 1910, instituted a Repertory Season at the Duke of York's Theatre. The plays given were Shaw's *Misalliance*, Galsworthy's *Justice*, Granville Barker's *The Madras House*, Barrie's *The Twelve Pound Look*, and Pinero's *Trelawney of the Wells*. The Abbey Theatre, Dublin, did some admirable pioneering, attacking Manchester in full force in April, 1906. In two evenings the company gave performances of Synge's *The Shadow of the Glen* and *Riders to the Sea*, Yeats's *Cathleen ni Houlihan* and *Pot of Broth*, Lady Gregory's *Spreading the News* and William Boyle's *The Building Fund*. The *Manchester Guardian*, representing all that the Manchester intelligentsia which does not go to the play might be supposed to think if it did, received the invaders with such enthusiasm that Miss Horniman was emboldened to take over the old Comedy Theatre, rename it "The Gaiety," and start her famous venture in repertory. Prior to this she had been further encouraged by a successful performance at the Midland Theatre—an uncomfortable, incommodious hall in the Midland Hotel—of Shaw's *Widowers' Houses* and Charles McEvoy's *David Ballard*. In connection with this latter performance the *Manchester Guardian* wisely wrote:

"The Playgoers' Theatre made a fine beginning last night with two plays by Mr. Charles McEvoy, who has done very well this time, and may do even better presently. We need not acclaim his plays as masterpieces, for they are not quite that, and perhaps the interest of this new venture in Manchester will lie less in the repetition of acknowledged masterpieces than in these significant efforts of the younger men. It will be our privilege not merely to chronicle approval and congratulate author and actors on successes such as that of last night, but to share in the developments, to criticise, and to learn. The mistake would be to suppose that this theatre is to do something miraculous or stupendous, and to overshadow all that has gone before. To be chosen even of the Playgoers' Theatre does not imply inspirations of a new, exclusive kind. What we received from Mr. McEvoy was a notable attempt to bring the theatre nearer to our lives; but like others, he is struggling with technical difficulties; hesitating, perhaps, between the influence of the greater dramatists who have written before him and the spectacle as he sees it, but always with a good eye for the human type, and for those moments when hidden things boil to the surface and the years are illuminated in the moment. Altogether the occasion was stimulating, and Mr. McEvoy and the Playgoers' Theatre scored a success that should hearten them in their work. We felt that if we were saving our country it was quite a delightful way to do it. Perhaps some of us were almost more anxious about the audience than about the plays, for we have a secret anxiety that Manchester, as well as the Playgoers' Theatre, should come out of the affair with credit. Happily all went well, and appreciation was most heartily expressed."

The best work of the Manchester Repertory Company was done between 1907 and 1912, rather less good work between 1912 and 1915.

A glance at the programmes shows a number of performances of:

Hippolytus . . .	Euripides
The Trojan Women .	Euripides
Measure for Measure .	W. Shakespeare
The Comedy of Errors	W. Shakespeare
Every Man in his Humour	Ben Jonson
She Stoops to Conquer.	Oliver Goldsmith
The School for Scandal	R. B. Sheridan
Man and Superman .	George Bernard Shaw
Major Barbara . .	George Bernard Shaw
The Voysey Inheritance	Granville Barker
Prunella	Laurence Housman and Granville Barker
The Silver Box .	John Galsworthy
The Pigeon . .	John Galsworthy
The Cloister . .	Emile Verhaeren
The Tragedy of Nan	John Masefield
David Ballard . .	Charles McEvoy
Hindle Wakes . .	Stanley Houghton

Indeed, no type of drama, ancient or modern, was omitted from the programmes, all the plays receiving adequate staging and good, careful, if not always brilliant interpretation by the actors.

Criticism of repertory acting must always labour under great difficulties. That incomparable prig in the play, Pryce Ridgeley, was astonished, in view of the stipends of the minor clergy, "to get the Gospel preached as satisfactorily as we do." Repertory acting is middling absolutely and good relatively. It is good "considering." And the explanation is simple. A Repertory Theatre is known to exist for the production of plays which cannot get a hearing on the commercial stage, *i.e.* which cannot draw a house. In that fore-knowledge a house refuses to be drawn, which is what somebody meant by declaring action and reaction to be equal and opposite. Hence the employment, at modest salaries, of "repertory" actors, by which one means a celebrity on the down-grade or a humble person who has never climbed. It is not implied that these actors act any the worse for being paid small money or that the commercial actor acts any better for being paid big money. It should be evident, however, that fashionable players adjudged by public opinion to be good actors, and great players who have forced public opinion to follow in their wake, are able to command higher salaries than a Repertory Theatre can afford. So the Repertory Theatre has to take what is left. At the same time it must be stated definitely that to the credit of the Gaiety Theatre we must put many pieces of acting which were absolutely as well as relatively fine.

Throughout all these years it was a case of pull Horniman pull Cotton-Merchant. And the merchant won by sheer force of inertia.

The Gaiety Theatre, playing to smaller and smaller houses and consequently bigger and bigger losses, had to close down shortly after the war. It is now a Picture Palace, and Manchester stupidity once more breathes freely. I count Miss Horniman's Gaiety enterprise as second to the Vedrenne-Barker venture at the Court Theatre in the great dramatic revival in this country which began with the opening of the present century and is still going on. I must, at this point, drop the intellectual theatre for a space and return to the commercial stage.

SHAW

Here is now a tale of two sorts of ardour, the fiery exaltation of the modern school breaking new ground without having practised upon the old, and the heroism of the old gang, including the indefatigable Alfred Sutro and charming Hubert Henry Davies, bringing its work into line with the new spirit. The giant of the period is obviously Bernard Shaw. Many critics have written volumes round this great writer, some to explain him, others to explain him away. Many minds have told us what we ought to think about Shaw, who has devoted large tracts of his own writings to telling us what he thinks about himself. Professor Allardyce Nicoll sums up as succinctly as anybody when he says:

"The keynotes to Mr. Shaw's work are intellect and rebellion. Whatever is sentimental and romantic he despises as false. Whatever is contrary to the dictates of reason he opposes. Whatever is set up as a fetish by the unthinking mass he ruthlessly destroys. His socialism is not of the emotional kind. He is not inspired with a great pity for 'the under dog' as Mr. Galsworthy is. Rather does he look round him, and, witnessing the many follies in our management of life, he strives to remedy the abuses, not by serious problem plays, but by turning topsy-turvy our social stage. . . . Complacency and romantic artificiality are his *bêtes noires*. He objects to the typical assumptions of the sentimental dramatists just as much as he objects to the typical assumptions of the sentimentalists in real life. Everything, therefore, comes within the sphere of his caustic pen—literature, art, medicine, religion, politics, racial prejudice, social standards. He is the great destroyer of evil in our modern age, and out of his destructiveness we are led toward a newer, fresher, and more constructive thought."

I shall not enumerate the plays of this writer. Readers ought to know the titles of Shaw's plays, and what they are about; if they don't their local book-seller will tell them.

GALSWORTHY

Next in point of consequence we may put Galsworthy—"honest John" as he ought to be called. Shaw is the intellectual pioneer worrying speculation with pick and shovel, Galsworthy the orderer of such thought as we already possess. The one is all "flash and outbreak of a fiery mind," the other is a lamp of pity. Mr. Galsworthy is a moderate of the utmost violence, holding a middle line as meticulously as a drunken man. He sees that two is the minimum number of sides to any case, and where he is content with two, gives you a carefully measured six of one and an exact half-dozen of the other. His plays are all about men in the street, shop or office and through them all we hear the cry: "But for the Grace of God there goes John Galsworthy!"

This writer is in himself an entire Humane Society. He sides with the fox against the man in pink, the hen-coop against the marauding fox, the chickweed against the chicken, and whatever it is the chickweed preys on against that ferocious plant. You might say that his pity comes too easily and is inclined to resemble a bath-room tap which has been left running. But even so it is less irritating than the saturated sweetness of Barrie. Which of the two is the second playwright of our time is a matter which I shall not attempt to determine. The book-seller who obliged with the list of Shaw's plays will doubtless do the same for Galsworthy.

DRINKWATER

We now come to the case of Drinkwater, whose stock in the English theatre is considerably lower than it ought to be. One feels that this is largely due to the fact that this playwright has, doubtless *malgré lui*, imposed upon the public some impression of priggishness. He is too obviously out to improve our minds, morals and manners.

In his preface to the very handsome collection of his plays the author makes complaint of the waywardness of certain of his critics. It is not our business, he asserts, to tell him that

Lincoln, Cromwell, and Lee were this, that and the other thing which the plays were not meant to indicate. "The fact that I have not shown these men as some things that they were is of no consequence; criticism's part is to point out anything essential that I have shown them to be which they were not." And Drinkwater goes on to claim that if he has succeeded in dramatising the idea without falsifying the character, he has fulfilled his intention.

What is the essential "idea" in all the more important works of this playwright? Obviously the idea of leadership. Let our author explain this in his own words:

> "There was the man who, certain of his aims, had to face all the cunning and malice of unscrupulous intrigue in order to preserve what he conceived to be the only sure foundations of society as he knew it. This was leadership determined to preserve a great establishment. There was then the man who was convinced that society as he knew it was being destroyed by corruption and tyranny, and who was determined with a religious zeal to sweep away the old order and found a new one. Then again, there was the leader who felt, with absolute

purity of heart, that loyalty to his own tradition was the first, and altogether becoming duty of man. Here, then, were the three aspects of my problem, or perhaps one should say three of the aspects: the leader inspired by a great moral idea to the vindication of a system, the leader inspired by a great moral idea to the overthrow of a system, and the leader for whom a system became a great moral idea in itself."

Our author goes on to claim that since his intention was not the exhaustive presentation of a character, but the dramatisation of a theme, he was entitled to take or reject such elements of character as he chose. But does not Mr. Drinkwater realise that the ordinary man, who must master the plays without the assistance of a spiritual crib, may very well mistake the riddle sifting a man's leadership from his less admirable qualities for the bucket of whitewash covering him from head to foot? Drinkwater labels a character Lincoln, *tout court*, from which the average playgoer must necessarily deduce an essay in truth as the police-court understands that virtue. It may be of supreme artistic unimportance that Lincoln liked a good smoke-room story, that

Cromwell was frowsy in personal habit, and that Lee degenerated into a schoolmaster. But surely if a writer leads one to believe in him as a biographer he should be the complete biographer exhibiting the blemishes of his subject in all their relative unimportance. One grants, of course, the right of any artist to use historical characters as pegs and nothing but pegs, provided he makes good his artist's claim to move in a world apart from the biographer's.

But Drinkwater has in places dealt so faithfully by his characters, even to the using of their historically recorded words, that the reader or spectator looks to him willy-nilly as to a Boswell. This is awkward, since this writer now tells us that his aim was to play the Shakespeare and the Shaw. It would be a foolish objection to Shakespeare's Brutus to say that his author omitted to state that he was a moneylender who did business with Cicero at ten per cent. The point is that Shakespeare poured into Brutus as much of himself as that character would contain, and then a good deal more. The same thing is true of Shaw as Joan. Now comes Drinkwater specifically claiming the right to spill himself equally into Lincoln and Mary Stuart, and our author is distinctly cross because a Scottish educational journal suggested that somebody ought to send him some books about that Queen. Probably no historian will easily accept the apology which is contained in Mary's desire "to see strong children about me, to play with an easy, festival mind, to walk the evenings at peace." This, surely, is to show Mary as something which the balance of historical judgment has decided that she was not. It is all very well to snatch up the poor creatures of this earth and transfigure them in the light of one's own nobility. But where is the thing to stop? Drinkwater announces a play on Robert Burns in which he will show a hitherto unattempted complexity of character, and we hear that he is about to dramatise the life of Byron. Are we to see his new heroes as men, or as illustrations of the love for humanity and other people's freedom? How would our author use Parnell or St. Paul?

The real question is: Does Drinkwater bring to his work sufficient imaginative reality to justify, without advertisement, his theory of dramatic significance? Perhaps one may say without unkindness that this imaginative reality is discovered to be there as soon as we are told to look for it.

But re-perusal of these plays does definitely

show them to be the work of a poet, the texture of whose mind is definitely noble. This playwright has at least loved the highest sufficiently to seize upon it wherever he has found it and to turn it into a play. Many poets, one agrees, have written dramas which are immortal by virtue of some quality which does not belong to the stage, plays which have made up for lack of action by abundance of spiritual conflict. It can never be said of Drinkwater's drama that it wants anything in the latter respect; and of action there is, for the sane mind, surely enough and to spare. It is generally accepted that one play at least by Shaw will become part of the dateless and fashionless inheritance of the English stage. Is it too much to predict that the theatre which shall in future ages retain sufficient nobility to produce *St. Joan* will not ignore *Abraham Lincoln*? One would lay it down without hesitation that Drinkwater's masterpiece will endure.

BARKER

Next in importance—leaving on one side for the moment the master of the whimsical and the poetic—is Harley Granville Barker. Barker's plays, of which the best is *The Voysey Inheritance*, are not so much plays as conversations. The author will button-hole you for four mortal hours and at his best is good, second-rate Shaw, which is a good deal higher than first-rate anybody else. Barker's plays, of which several have been published, are:

The Weather Hen (with Berte Thomas) (1899)
The Marrying of Ann Leete (1902)
A Miracle (1902)
Prunella (with Laurence Housman) (1904)
The Voysey Inheritance (1905)
Waste (1907)
The Madras House (1910)
Rococo (1911)
The Harlequinade (with D. C. Calthrop) (1914)
Vote by Ballot (1914)
Farewell to the Theatre (1916)
The Secret Life (1923)

Something will be said later concerning *Our Betters*, the best known work of W. Somerset Maugham. Like Pinero, this brilliant playwright has, when writing for the stage, no interest in any humanity which does not possess at least three thousand a year and a flat in Curzon Street. His technique is flawless and *The Circle* is his best play. The works of this most accomplished craftsman are as follows:

A Man of Honour (1903)
Lady Frederick (1907)
The Explorer (1908)
Jack Straw (1908)
Mrs. Dot (1908)
Penelope (1909)
Smith (1909)
The Tenth Man (1910)
Landed Gentry (1910)
Loaves and Fishes (1911)
The Land of Promise (1914)
Caroline (1916)
The Unattainable (1916)
Our Betters (1917)
Love in a Cottage (1918)
Cæsar's Wife (1919)
Home and Beauty (1919)
The Unknown (1920)
The Circle (1921)
East of Suez (1922)
The Camel's Back (1924)

HANKIN

And now we must go back a little and take a glance at the Manchester school, which began with St. John Hankin though that distinguished dramatist never, to my knowledge, set foot in that sad city. But he did set foot in Berwick-upon-Tweed, the occasion being the first performance of *The Return of the Prodigal*. The date was the middle of November, 1906, and how much the New Drama was in the air, and the amount of importance attached to it, may be gauged by the fact that the local dramatic critic was allowed to spill himself over three columns. This piece of criticism has offered me so much entertainment during the last twenty years that I feel I cannot deny my readers a taste of it, and even a goodly slice. Here it is:

"'I Have Played the Triangle.' These are the words of the Prodigal himself in the course of his disclosure of his experiences among the Flotsam and the Jetsam of the World. And this, to us, seems to sum up, in fair measure, Mr. St. J. Hankin's clever new play of sunshine and shadow, which was so successfully staged at the Queen's Rooms Theatre, Berwick.

"What does Mr. St. J. Hankin, who himself came down from London Town to Berwick for this important event in the annals of the Border Stage, essay? Briefly, he deals out, as all properly built authors ought to deal out, that ever-engrossing card yclept Humanity. The thing is in a nutshell—an eminently respectable family—as families go—has its Prodigal. The boy—probably, after all is said and done, the best, at bottom, of the whole bunch in the Family—is shipped off to Australia to save the Family honour, forsooth; and he inconveniently returns. And there you have a peg quite strong enough upon which to hang securely not only one play but a thousand sound plays and a thousand useful lessons.

"It's an old tale this—'Lost to Sight, Lost

to Mind'—this eminently respectable family moving in apparently good circles, has got rid of its Skeleton—its 'Prodigal,' and they thank Heaven—in their peculiar way—that is by saying nothing—for their good luck. But, 'The Mills of God Grind Slowly, but They Grind Exceeding Small'; and the Prodigal comes home again at the usual inconvenient time—at least for this eminently respectable, presumably God-fearing Family. How true it all is to Nature—to Everyday Life!

"Act I. introduces us to the usual social round of 'So-Pleased-to-Meet-You,' nothingnesses, and the well-known common-place sayings and doings of the Prodigal's eminently respectable neighbours. Scarce a word is mentioned of the Prodigal—"Blood of Their Blood, Flesh of Their Flesh, and Bone of Their Bone"—but, just as the storm-cloud no bigger than a man's hand comes up on the horizon and develops into a rain-storm and a gale and a blizzard, so back, inopportunely, comes the Prodigal to the home of his Father. And where better right has he to come? Let the mother that bore him and the father that rejoiced in his birth say!

"So, with Act I, Mr. St. J. Hankin brings the Prodigal Home, like a Thunderclap, to the bosom of his eminently respectable Family, which was resting, as it thought, in the cosy Lap of Security; and Home he comes to knock topsy-turvy all calculations, and to set most of his precious dear relatives afloat on the ocean of Discontent and Discord. It is, we have heard, very unpleasant, thoroughly unsatisfactory, and most annoying, to have undesirable relatives, but once out of the way these undesirable relatives have a peculiar knack—a bad habit—of turning up when they are not wanted. How many of us, thank Heaven, get through the World without being found out! Still, we probably shall be found out in the next World if we are so really lucky to escape detection on this Terrestrial Globe!

"We are inclined to think that Mr. St. J. Hankin, who is undoubtedly an able Playwright, prolongs Act 1; and, thereby, in our opinion, the curtain suffers. Curtains are most important things in a Play. Had we been writing *The Return of the Prodigal*, we fancy we would have worked up, with all the intensity possible, to the actual carrying in and laying down on the sofa of the Prodigal Son; and then we might have made it the point for the other son —the schemer, the respectable Prodigal, who is at profitable peace with his rich and well-placed parents—to have said 'Father, it is he who has disgraced us.' Whereupon, remembering the beautiful words of one of our most beautiful hymns:

> Can a woman's tender care
> Cease towards the child she bare?

the mother, ever-forgiving, might assuredly say, with the utmost dramatic fervour, 'My son, my son,' then embrace him and cry, 'Thank God for his safe return Home,' faint right away, and—Curtain! And, in our opinion, an intensely dramatic curtain, too—a thunderclap, nothing more nor less.

"Act 2, as might be expected from a serious Dramatist, leads us on to the question as to what is to be done with the non-respectable Prodigal—the Undesirable—though, mark you, St. J. Hankin's Prodigal is, we consider, worthy of a better fate than awaits him. The Prodigal is not so black as he is painted: none of us are. Are we? But, the sanctimonious son of the Jacksons who has his eye on the main chance—on social prestige, on his father's help, and on the girl Stella Faringford, daughter of a real, live Baronet—doesn't want the Prodigal—son of the same mother, his own father's child—

and his own love for Stella arouses, as does the Winter's wind the sea out yonder in Berwick Bay, and increases violently, his hatred for his own brother; and so the Prodigal—barring the tender solicitude of his mother—comes in for rough handling, is storm-tossed like a frail craft; and a very good curtain falls on the Prodigal's emphatic decision that what he means to do, now that he has returned Home, is to 'Do Nothing!' And, under the circumstances, he is not altogether to be blamed.

"Act 3 leads us along in the Labyrinth of uncertainties, and the Prodigal, having to suit himself to his company, has to dissemble and become just as one of other Namby-Pambies; and so he sits tight, and when the first gong goes for dinner he philosophically decides that as the 'First gong has gone I shall go and dress for dinner.' Probably a youth of greater self-will and of more pronounced spirit and trained independence would have 'Gone Out Into the Night,' and told his People generally to go to the Devil, but—*cherchez la femme*—Stella Faringford is about, and herein is, perchance his undoing. Alas! ultimately he wins neither the girl nor his Family's affections, though he might, and he ought, to have won both, and his sanctimonious, humbugging brother, who is prepared to betray his own brother's confidences, ought to have been severely taught a lesson.

"Act 4 is the best of the quartette, and is responsible for a beautiful *tête-à-tête*—we refer to the scene between the sister and the Prodigal son. If the worldly father had been sane enough to realise it his daughter might have saved the Prodigal and restored him and rehabilitated him in the Family Circle. But, unfortunately, Père Jackson is a tool in his stay-at-home son's hands; and so, the Prodigal—without even a farewell to his best friend in the house—his own mother—goes back to the World, disowned—out into the black night—out to anywhere—to the devil if he likes—with £250 a year of an allowance. This allowance, by the way, is won by a clever stroke on the part of the Prodigal. In Act 3 he is disowned—cut off without a penny—by his father, for running up tailors' bills. 'Well, if I go,' he says, 'it will be to the nearest Workhouse'; and the Prodigal explains airily how this will ruin his father's Parliamentary ambitions and his brother's social ambitions. This brother, Henry, calls it 'a sordid plot,' but his Prodigal brother rightly attributes its success to the fact that 'His father is a Snob and his brother also a Snob.' However, as we have said, the Prodigal is bought with £250 a year, and out he goes from the Home—out to God knows where. . . ."

Whenever I think of Hankin's plays one scene crops up. It is the end of the second act of *The Charity that Began at Home.* Earlier in the act Lady Denison's butler, Soames, has declared that, being married, he is unable to make amends to the lady's maid whom he has betrayed. Lady Denison's charitable views incline her to retain the man in her service. And then Marjory Denison must needs become engaged to an undesirable! This is altogether too much for her mother, who says: "I don't mind asking the wrong people to my house and trying to make them happy, but I can't have them proposing to my daughter. I must make a stand against it all, now, at once, *while I remember*." She goes to the bell. "What are you going to do?" asks her sister. "*Dismiss Soames!*" There is all Hankin in this little episode. Hankin died in 1909 at the age of thirty-nine, and in him the English theatre lost one who showed every sign of becoming a master-craftsman. His plays, all of which have been published except *Thompson*, which was finished by George Calderon, are :

The Two Mr. Wetherbys (1903)
The Return of the Prodigal (1905)
The Charity that Began at Home (1906)
The Cassilis Engagement (1907)
The Last of the De Mullins (1908)
The Burglar Who failed (1908)
The Constant Lover (1912)
Thompson (1913)

" HINDLE WAKES "

Probably the playwright who will always be most closely identified with the Manchester school is Stanley Houghton, whose *Hindle Wakes* took first London and then Lancashire by storm. Written in the autumn of 1911, it was produced by Mr. Lewis Casson, Miss Horniman's then director, for the Stage Society at the Aldwych Theatre on June 16, 1912. Mr. Harold Brighouse writes in his preface to his complete edition of Houghton's plays: " Never, perhaps, have the dramatic critics lavished upon a new man's play such praise as they bestowed on *Hindle Wakes*, and it was plain that the matter could not rest with the two performances before the Stage Society. Mr. Cyril Maude offered a home at the Playhouse, and there, through a desperately hot summer, *Hindle Wakes* was played until, in September,

Mr. Maude required the Playhouse for himself, and the run was concluded, to houses increasingly crowded, at the Court Theatre. In Manchester, where it was played in November, 1912, its success was immediate, and new box office records were set up at the Gaiety Theatre. The subsequent career was exceptional: through 1913 five companies played *Hindle Wakes* in the provinces, breaking records at many theatres in Lancashire and Yorkshire. In December, 1912, it was produced by Mr. William Brady at the Maxine Elliott Theatre, New York, where, in spite of the acting of Mr. Herbert Lomas as Nathaniel Jeffcote, an otherwise ill-chosen cast was responsible for its failure. In February, 1913, however, with a reconstructed cast, still including Mr. Lomas, it proved so successful at the small Fine Arts Theatre, Chicago, that it was transferred for an extended run to a large theatre, the Olympic. The total number of performances from its first production to the time of Houghton's death is 1,838."

Another writer of the Manchester school is Allan Monkhouse whose mind has always been too fine for the coarse medium of the stage. The spiritual value of this exquisite writer's work is very great; whether it has lived in the raw, coarse air of the playhouse is another matter. Mr. St. John Ervine, whose Manchester is Belfast, is another writer who must be mentioned here. *Jane Clegg* (1913), a study of a commercial traveller, is one of the finest naturalistic plays of our time. It disposes finally of the theory that dramatic critics should not write plays. Henry Clegg's last speech is a superb revelation of greasy mentality and furtive soul. Here it is, and I include it for the sheer joy of setting down:

"I'm not a bad chap, really. I'm just weak. I'd be all right if I had a lot of money and a wife that wasn't better than I am . . . Oh, I know, Jane! You *are* better than I am. Any fool can see that! It doesn't do a chap much good to be living with a woman who's his superior, at least, not the sort of chap I am. I ought to have married a woman like myself, or a bit worse. That's what Kitty is. She's worse than I am, and that sort of makes me love her. It's different with you. I always feel mean here. Yes, I am mean. I know that; but it makes me meaner than I really am to be living with you."

Superb is not too fine a word for *Mixed Marriage* (1911), and those who have seen or read *John Ferguson* speak well of it. Among other realists must be mentioned Arnold Bennett, whose magnificent achievements as a novelist blind popular and critical opinion to his undoubted capacity as a playwright of common-sense. Then there is Elizabeth Baker who has gone to the quite poor classes and dull ordinary people for her material. *Chains* is easily her best play.

STEPHEN PHILLIPS

And now, I suppose, we must cast an eye on the poets. Of Stephen Phillips, who, quite astonishingly, comes within our period, I can only think that his work, pretty and demoded as the Albert Memorial, is entirely forgotten. As a matter of purely antiquarian interest I give a list of Phillips's plays:

Paolo and Francesca (1899)
Herod (1900)
Ulysses (1902)
The Sin of David (1904)
Aylmer's Secret (1905)
Nero (1906)
Faust (with J. Comyns Carr) (1908)
The Last Heir (1908)
Pietro of Siena (1910)
The King (1910)
Nero's Mother (1913)
The Adversary (1913)
Armageddon (1915)
Harold (1916)

MASEFIELD

A poet of an entirely different order is John Masefield, one of the best writers of our time, yet whose works hardly ever get on to the stage and once on do not succeed in holding it. Can this be because he is, in the words of Mr. Ashley Dukes, "a bough torn from the spirit of his time?" *The Tragedy of Nan* is undoubtedly this author's finest play. On the occasion of its performance by Miss Horniman's company at the Gaiety Theatre, Manchester, C. E. Montague wrote:

"'Nan' is of good family; it comes of the stock of the Elizabethan pastoral tragedy and has a coarse ancestor in the pseudo-Shakespeare *Yorkshire Tragedy* and a noble one in the close of *King John*, where the King dies, poisoned, in the orchard. Mr. Masefield has set his tragedy in one of those Hesperidean counties of West England where wind-fallen apples float whole sunny afternoons in the lazy pools above mill-dams. No place could help him more to gain the contrast which pastoral tragedy seeks between the momentary poignancy of its action and the perennial peace and geniality of a framing outward world. The landscape, too, is no mere dab or two of local colour in stage directions; it possesses the minds of his chief characters as the sea possesses Synge's people in *Riders to the Sea*, and the hill pastures in *The Shadow of the Glen*, so that the more impassioned they grow, the more naturally do they talk of it, as people brought up to church-going begin to interject about God when moved.

"Like Synge, again, Mr. Masefield has an unsentimental sympathy with his rustics; he studies peasant cruelty without either raging at it or idealising it into something else, and he works it into his picture without brutalising the picture's general tone; he has, also, something of Synge's skill in picking the queer little concrete details which give description vividness, like Nan's imagination of her drowned body 'knockin' agen the bridges,' and something of his wise wildness of figurative speech in passages of passion; and he has an ear for the rhythms of the living voice—he neither gives simple people strings of nubbly polysyllables to mouth nor the bastard semi-metrical stuff in which half our dramatists, in scenes of attempted emotion, ape the dithering whine of fiddlestrings that usually supports them on such occasions. We are not quite sure whether he has always succeeded in keeping the taint of 'literariness' out of his dialogue—for example where Nan says that she 'was a fly in the spider's web and the web came round me and round me till it was a shroud.' Once or twice such passages left us hesitating—was Mr. Masefield the man of letters planting upon Nan an accepted literary phrase, or was Mr. Masefield the observer of life seeking to convey the special quality of pathos that comes when an untaught mind, striving for fuller self-expression in a moment of exaltation, lays hands on some old flower of speech cast off by the more affluent? But of the beauty of the play as a whole, and especially of its central character, there can be no doubt."

Mr. Masefield's plays, which everybody reads with admiration and nobody ever gets the chance of going to see, are:

The Campden Wonder (1907)
The Tragedy of Nan (1908)
Mrs. Harrison (1909)
The Tragedy of Pompey the Great (1910)
Philip the King (1914)
The Faithful (1915)
The Locked Chest (1916)
The Sweeps of Ninety-Eight (1916)
Good Friday (1916)
A King's Daughter (1923)
Melloney Holtspur (1923)

SUGAR AND SPICE

From the poetic to the whimsical is only a step, and the step takes us at once to the plays of J. M. Barrie. I shall beg leave to reproduce a few sentences from a book of my own which was beautifully published, handsomely unread, and is now decently forgotten. It was in *At Half-Past Eight* that I wrote:

"Once there was a mother star gathered little baby stars round her knee to tell them a fairy story, and during the telling the genius of Barrie was born. For genius it is, despite a passion for literary baby-ribbons only too easily parodied. You could never mistake *Dear Brutus*, recently revived at Wyndham's Theatre, for the accretion of a talent, however industrious. The rarer attribute is written all over it, not very large perhaps, but in the authentic hand-writing. The essence of genius is its power to achieve without pains. That *tour de force* of Jupiter's, the birth of Minerva, was the trick, unrehearsed and inimitable. None but the old gentleman would have thought of it. It is surely the hall-mark of genius that its fruits, but for their creator, had never been thought of. Talent plods, and its outcome will be stumbled upon sooner or later, if not by the first explorer, then by another. A later than Newton would have questioned the falling apple, a second Stephenson drawn deductions from his kettle. Einstein merely anticipated by a week or a century the inevitable discovery that nothing's white or black but relativity makes it so. In the world of talent it is 'dogged as does it.' In the world of genius it is dogged as doesn't.

"To come to our little organism called the theatre. Can it be doubted that if Sir Arthur Pinero or Mr. John Drinkwater had turned their great talents away from the stage, we should still have had *The Second Mrs. Tanqueray* and *Abraham Lincoln*? Their epochs reeked with these plays. Non-existent, their temper was in the air. If St. Paul had lived in the 'nineties he would have pursued the lady with whips, scorpions, and perhaps an even fuller understanding; regenerate, he would have mouthed those melancholy confidences, enlivening them, it may be, with a dash of the original Saul. But he would never, we must think, have hit upon Peter Pan or the boy who 'bit his warts and politely swallowed the blood.' Not even a greater genius can recapture the lost spirit of a lesser. Hartmann defines this quality as 'the spontaneous manifestation of the untrammelled soul,' but then he was a German. To the non-Teutonic mind it is obvious that genius must take some pains; it were inspired lunacy else. So Beethoven tinkers incessantly at his themes, with the result that after twenty years he has whittled his chromatic glory down to the diatonic monotony apt for the plastering of Schiller's 'Ode to Joy.' Contrariwise we find Dickens hammering a grotesque name on the anvil till he has forged the apparently inspired 'Chuzzlewit.' Like these, Barrie is no wander-wit, but a master-contriver. His soul, as Herbert says, may be divinely loose about him, but he makes fast with the shrewdest nails such bits of it as he uses. Yet it is only the form of the conceit which he fashions into shape; the raw material of felicity springs from his brain flushed with ultimate delight.

"A reviewer of the early *Little Minister* wrote, 'The reader is held spell-bound, not by any cunningly devised artifices, but by the sympathy which is evoked in his breast.' That which held the reviewer spell-bound was, of course, the sympathy overflowing in the writer's breast. Sir James himself has said a good deal on this matter of sympathy. The Dominie asks Sentimental Tommy how he managed to write the passage about the willow hanging over the grave. 'I thought I was Betsy at the time,' answered Tommy. 'She told me nothing about the willow,' countered Mr. Cathro. 'You hadna speired if there was one,' the boy retorted. There you have both the natural gift, and the painstaker's looking before and after. 'Oh, you jewel!' cried Mr. Ogilvy, when Tommy lost the essay prize through excessive deliberation over the just word. 'He *had* to think of it till he got it. The laddie is a genius!' Which looks as though Sir James held, as they say, with *Ecclefechan*. The word was at the back of Tommy's mind all the time; the infinity of pains was used to bring it to the surface. The peculiar genius of Barrie, as playwright, consists in his knack of bringing from the back of his mind the simple things which lie behind the mind of the spectator. They are the things which, but for the twist of kindly laughter, would be unbearable. For the same reason Barrie prefers sentimentality to sentiment because it hurts less. Fortitude, irony even, are plants too prickly for his tender world. To keep young is the great adventure; old age and death are but dream-disasters. 'To be very gay is so near to being very sad,' is as near to actuality as Sir James will venture. I know of no other writer who has burked life so exquisitely."

These, then, are the dramatists—Shaw, Galsworthy, Drinkwater, Barker, Maugham, Hankin, Houghton, Monkhouse, Ervine, Masefield and Barrie—who brought about the renaissance of the English drama between the years 1900 and 1914.

SUCCESSORS TO ROBERTSON

The point about them all is that they brought the drama into touch with the common facts of life, as those facts were stirring in the general mind in the early years of the present century. They were really doing, only in a much more profound manner and on a bigger scale, what Robertson did in the 'sixties. But the most distinguished playwright cannot till a field unless the field is there to till, and Messrs. J. T. Grein, Vedrenne, Barker, Charrington, the inaugurators of the Stage Society, Sir Barry Jackson and Miss Horniman were pioneers who provided the field for new thought to break up. Then came the war, and with it a flood of light entertainment in most cases æsthetically worthless. One would be wrong to sneer at this; these light entertainments fulfilled admirably the need of the times. The minds as well as the bodies of the tired soldiery needed relaxation. Men back from the trenches wanted no further enlightenment as to the facts of life; they had experienced certain of them and knew that these could be hard enough. What they wanted was pure fancy and pure sentiment. They got a plentiful supply of both, and pure foolishness did not come amiss. The difficulty arose when the war came to an end and the theatres were still very largely in the hands of money-makers who knew nothing whatever about the art of the drama and cared less. Speculators had come into the business in immense numbers, ready to throw away five or ten thousand pounds on the off-chance of making fifty or a hundred thousand; and of these speculators there was apparently an inexhaustible supply. And as it is a matter of general knowledge that nothing in the English theatre has ever made large fortunes except rubbish, it was upon rubbish that the speculative mind was singly bent. About this time there was produced one of the most brilliant plays which has ever fallen from the pen of an English dramatist. Somerset Maugham's *Our Betters*, which had created an enormous sensation in

America, was produced in London with immediate and immense success. It is a magnificent piece of satire, and the work of a master of the theatre.

I can only repeat what I have said in another place that this was a comedy of manners which depicted what the author himself would probably admit to be only a very small section of society. Here again was the old picture of well-bred immorality lit up by flashes of hard, conscienceless, compunctionless wit. Mr. Maugham's characters, like those of Congreve, confessed their narrow interest in life, and flitted before us, as we have heard so often, without impinging upon our moral sense. Their meanness and vulgarity amused us a little, perhaps; these qualities had certainly no power to offend. You do not ask whether a butterfly conforms to a moral standard; you pin it down and try not to destroy the bloom upon its wings. Mr. Maugham secured a very brilliant specimen in Lady George Grayston, and with her capture enriched that national collection which has come down to us from the Restoration.

The play was really extraordinarily deft, and its matter was handled with any amount of "style." Think, for a moment, of the way in which heavier-handed, more "sincere" playwrights would have treated that cold, calculating blonde, Lady George Grayston, that lightning calculator with the air of an inconscient featherbrain. Is it to be imagined that Mr. Sutro, for example, would have been content to leave her at the end in perfect poise upon her brazen pinnacle? Would not that husband of hers, whom Mr. Maugham kept so adroitly in London out of discovery's way, have come trumpeting to Grayston, razed those improper towers and hauled the châtelaine off to Alaska, or some abode of Arctic chastity? Would not Sir Arthur Pinero have plunged her into suicide on the discovery that some day she must grow old and that :

> With the coming of the crow's-feet
> Goes the backward turn of beaux' feet?

Would not Mr. Henry Arthur Jones have probed beneath that brassy bosom to a heart of gold? Would not Wilde have let off innumerable squibs round a bonfire of sodden sentiment till the playhouse resembled a smoky backyard on a wet Fifth?

How would any one of these playwrights have treated that dark and common beauty, the Duchesse de Surennes, divided between passion and parsimony, torn between her sentiment—forgive the word—for Gilbert Paxton and that blackguard's drain upon her purse? Would not Sir James Barrie have discovered the "mother-instinct" in disguise? Would not that eager gardener, Mr. George Bernard Shaw, have exterminated her and her kind with three acts of weed-killer, maximum strength? And would not Mr. Galsworthy have found fresh cause for pity? Mr. Arnold Bennett. . . . But perhaps the people who do not matter are not this writer's world.

All these are fine playwrights, yet I cannot conceive that they would have held themselves so icily detached and aloof from their miserable creatures as did Mr. Maugham. Any one of them—and I will add for this purpose the late Haddon Chambers—might have put together that excellent second act, the "great" scene in which the impudent lady is surprised with the Duchess's lover. But would they—I do not say could they—have kept the "situation" so rigorously on the plane of heartlessness? Would there not have been question of sentiment?

It seems a parodoxical thing to say, but probably the play would have been even finer if it had been shorn of its two honest characters, the little American back-woodsman or great-heart from the candy-store—a creation, this, after Mr. Sutro's own fancy—and the sentimentalising Principessa, a romantic creature whose marriage to a foreign prince had apparently been brought about by a too-persistent perusal of the "Songs before Sunrise" and the Italian Debrett. These two brought a blurring to the hard lines of the picture, translated us to a world where decency was, and so suggested questions of moral censure.

THE NAUGHTY PLAYWRIGHTS

Really one does not know whether to regard Maugham's play as a blessing or a curse. For this first-class work of a brilliant mind found imitators possessed of the brilliance without the mentality. In plain English it was largely responsible for the flood of dismal and dreary lubricity which at once began to swamp the English stage. Not that the lubricity was dull and dismal to begin with. First there was young and clever Mr. Noel Coward firing off like minute-guns brilliant plays in which nymphomaniac mothers drove their sons to dope, and the wives of stock-brokers took to tippling at the dinner-table prior to toppling on the sofa. Mr. Frederick Lonsdale followed suit with plays in which (*a*) the sweeping of the domestic hearth was entrusted to the sweepings of the streets and (*b*) pearl thieves achieved the prodigious in the way of the magnanimous and the genteel. The slope in English play-writing was precipitous and the decline swift. At the foot of it were to be found the plays of Mr. Michael Arlen and Sir Patrick Hastings, whose characters were trash and whose atmosphere was that of the so-called beauty-parlour. In plays of this type silliness and offensiveness reached their high-water mark, and the fact that they were instantaneously successful shows English taste at its lowest ebb. I do not say that bawdiness should have no place in art; it has a place and a very good place too. But I do object, as I think all reasonable people must object, to a flux of plays in which the characters have no other reason for existence except their lewdness. The difference between Mr. Maugham and his successors is that whereas he is a playwright with an immense interest in life who chooses to exhibit one side of it for what it is, the others give you the impression that the whole world is composed of vicious babies, and that nobody who has grown up is worth writing about.

If all the people represented by the characters in the plays of Messrs. Coward, Lonsdale, Arlen and Company were put into a bag and drowned in the Thames the intellectual and industrial, artistic and social world of London would not be one whit the poorer. It is useless to tell the begetters of these characters that they are not of use; one wonders whether they can be made to see that they are not polite, and that the world they move in is ill-bred. Yet I feel sure that this wave of vulgarity will pass. It has already deleted the West-End theatre from among those things in which any rational person can take interest. Always, of course, with exceptions. And it is a commonplace that these plays hold no interest for the millions outside what Sir Arthur Pinero used to call "our little parish of St. James's."

THE SITUATION TO-DAY

This, then, is the situation in 1926. A large part of the London theatre is given up to plays about dope fiends and jazz-maniacs; other large tracts are abandoned to the inanities of musical comedy. Roughly speaking, three-fourths of the London stage is closed to persons possessed of the slightest particle of intellect or the least feeling for the drama. Picture theatres are springing up all over the place, attracting immense numbers of playgoers by their cheapness, superior comfort and the greater intellectual content of their programmes. Yet—and this is the thing I want most to say—there never was a time when the general interest in, and preoccupation with, the drama was bigger both in London and throughout the country. The spirit which made the Vedrenne-Barker venture possible not only still persists to-day, but has increased ten-fold. Twelve years ago there was one intellectual theatre in London; to-day there are half-a-dozen. Mr. McDermott, at the Everyman Theatre, Hampsteady, put up a very gallant fight for some years, hardly ever producing anything that was not good and never producing anything known by him to be æsthetically bad. That his venture was not a financial success was due to the fact that his theatre never became really fashionable, that the lift at the Hampstead tube is of all lifts the longest, and that the Londoner will talk about the intellectual drama, form societies to propagate it, and do anything and everything except go to it. Next, perhaps, we might mention Mr. Nigel

Playfair, at Hammersmith, who, having launched Mr. Drinkwater, seemed to lose interest in living playwrights, preferring rather to encourage those who have been dead a hundred years. In any case, for the past few years his eighteenth-century entertainments at the Lyric have been the delight and the rage of cultivated London taste. Mr. Ridgeway, at his little theatre at Barnes, re-discovered Tchehov, the Russian playwright, handsomely recognised as first-class by every other country except this. It may be that Mr. Ridgeway took a leaf out of Mr. Playfair's book, for it must be remembered that it was the Hammersmith production of *The Cherry Orchard* which set the Russian fashion. But the thing, of course, is to take the right leaf out of the right book, and Mr. Ridgeway deserves all the praise which one can shower upon him. "Curiouser and curiouser," as Alice remarked, even Ibsen came in for something which not even the greatest detractors of that master could call odium, both *The Wild Duck* and *A Doll's House* running for a number of weeks and to, all things considered, not very extravagant losses. Sir Barry Jackson, at the Court Theatre and elsewhere, succeeded in drawing a large metropolitan congregation to hear the gospel which at Birmingham he had preached with apostolic fervour. Miss Lena Ashwell, with three companies of players radiating from the Century Theatre, Notting Hill, has proved that playgoers in search of reasonable plays do not need to leave the suburbs. At King's Cross, Mr. Charles Macdona's company of moderately good actors have done sufficiently well with a repertoire devoted exclusively to Shaw to continue in possession of the Regent Theatre for many months in succession, while on the other side of the water Miss Baylis has continued to fill the Old Vic from floor to ceiling. But theatrical fashion is a kittle thing. Shout from the top of your voice to fashionable folk that a masterpiece by a world-famed author is to be performed within a stone's throw of Piccadilly Circus and you cannot get two people into the house; whisper to them that it will be performed at some hole-and-corner, out-of-the-way theatre, and that a pilgrimage is the smart thing, and the road will become impassable owing to the Rolls-Royces. But even in the very heart of the London commercial theatre much goodness and virtue have been found. Miss Sybil Thorndike and her devoted husband, Mr. Lewis Casson, took off a good thumping drawing-room melodrama with which they were coining money to put on, with sinking hearts and dithering knees, Mr. Shaw's *St. Joan*. The result, as all the world knows, was that they made still more money. Mr. Frederick Harrison continued to make the Haymarket Theatre a centre of polite plays for the polite world, of which Mr. Milne's *The Dover Road* may perhaps be considered a typical specimen. It was at this theatre that Mr. Harrison produced *The Man with a Load of Mischief*, by Mr. Ashley Dukes, a charming piece for the few which was taken quite unexpectedly to the bosom of the many. At the St. Martin's Theatre, Mr. Basil Dean spared no expense of judgment and cash in giving the public good English plays and good translations. One would mention particularly *A Bill of Divorcement* by Miss Clemence Dane, *The Likes of Her* by Mr. Charles McEvoy, and *R.U.R.* by Karel Capek. It was largely owing to Mr. Dean's enterprise and enthusiasm that Flekker's *Hassan* was, at long last, staged at His Majesty's. At the little Ambassadors, Captain H. M. Harwood produced many plays of interest, and at the Playhouse and the Adelphi Miss Gladys Cooper appeared in interesting revivals of *The Second Mrs. Tanqueray*, *Magda* and *Iris*. At the Pavilion Mr. Cochran produced revues which were always splendiferous and occasionally witty, and was, in addition, responsible for the visits of such notable foreign artists as Sarah Bernhardt, Eleonora Duse, the Guitrys, Cécile Sorel, Pauline Lord and the Chauve-Souris. In fact, one would say that the intelligent playgoer has been sure of intelligent entertainment within half-an-hour of Piccadilly Circus three nights in every week for the last five years.

THE SOCIETIES

I have said nothing up to now about the play-producing societies of which far away the most important is the Stage Society. The others put on a good play now and again to their own as well as everybody else's astonishment, but, in the main, they would appear to exist in order to sell at a profit commercial plays to commercial managers. These Sunday evening performances are an unmitigated nuisance to the dramatic critic, who sees far too many plays as it is and is deprived of the rest and recreation to which he, like everybody else, is entitled. Nine out of every ten plays produced on Sunday evening are limitlessly boring, yet the critic is bound to attend on the off-chance of finding something good. The generality of these productions consists of witless drivel dignified by the name of light comedy. The Sunday society was an admirable institution when it was forced into existence by the imbecilities of the censorship. Many of those imbecilities still remain, but the societies have ceased to be in any sense rebellious. They have become in great measure the champions of mental vacuity.

So far I have written entirely about London. But the whole point of this little essay is the insistence that there is an immense amount of interest in the drama outside London. Play-goers' clubs are in greater activity than ever before, there is more discussion of the drama than at any previous time, and more plays are being written. Again, London has broken down as a play centre from which travelling companies may be recruited. This is largely owing to the fact that the London theatre-goer likes a piece to be so short that it will interfere neither with a late dinner nor an early cabaret supper, and again because the provinces still in-dulge an old-fashioned predilection for heroines who are heroines and not street-walkers. The dearth of suitable plays has forced many provin-cial cities to follow the example of Manchester, which has turned its Theatre Royal, with a century of fame behind it—Irving was a member of its stock company—into a picture palace. But the hunger for drama still exists, and to satisfy it Repertory Theatres, I repeat, are springing up all over the country. I have already alluded to the fact that Miss Horniman's Repertory venture, Manchester, collapsed in 1919 or thereabouts. The Birmingham Repertory Theatre was started before the war by six enthusiasts meeting together in a private house under the leadership of Mr. Drinkwater and Sir Barry Jackson. This theatre has been responsible for the production of two hundred plays in eleven years, starting with the classical repertory of Shakespeare and Sheridan and going on through Ibsen to the most formidable of Shaw. On a level with the Birmingham Theatre is the Liverpool Playhouse, while other repertory theatres of note are those at Oxford, Hull, Newcastle-on-Tyne, Bristol and Southend-on-Sea. There are playgoers' clubs in Bath, Birmingham, Liverpool, Manchester, Nottingham, Sheffield and elsewhere. The Arts League of Service was founded in 1919, and with the object of bringing the arts into every-day life organised tours throughout England and part of Scotland. Every English county with the exception of Rutland has been visited. The first performance was given in May, 1919, when the company set out in a borrowed station wagonette on a fortnight's tour of the Sussex villages with a capital of £25. In six years this theatre has visited five hundred and fifty towns and villages, and travelled over twelve thousand miles. The wagonette has been returned to its owner, and is now replaced by a motor-car which carries a complete theatrical outfit. I shall not say much here about the British Drama League. The league by its constitution is debarred from taking any active part in the production of plays; and its work, about which everybody speaks very highly without perhaps knowing too exactly what it is, does not come within my scope.

THE AMATEURS

Neither am I greatly concerned with the amateur dramatic societies, of which there would appear to be one to every hundred members of the population. I want now to suggest to readers that they should disabuse their minds of the belief that the theatre in England is confined to Shaftesbury Avenue. The country teems with people who form themselves into dramatic societies moved by something deep down within them which one must call the creative spirit. Such an urge is not satisfied by witnessing plays or even by reading what the dramatic critics may have to say about new pieces in the London theatres. People who are really fond of music like to thump out for themselves some sort of tune on some sort of instrument. Browning declares his liking for the butcher who paints and the baker who rhymes, though he is careful to confine his admiration to the will to achieve. Frankly, I must say that I dislike amateur dramatic societies more than anything else in the world except, perhaps, amateur operatic societies. This for the simple reason that with a few rare exceptions I have never known any amateur actor who could act even when drawing a salary on the London professional stage. My unselfish view, however, is that it is as great a cruelty to keep people who want to act from acting as it is to keep budding musicians from strumming upon the piano. Amateur performance of the great masterpieces is excellent for the amateurs and the community. Anything less than masterpieces—light comedies, for example, which are only the parquet flooring for professional actors to polish—should be forbidden by law. Acting is a peculiar gift seldom encountered even in paid performers. Its simulation by amateurs fascinates me not at all, though on the moral score I cannot but admire the village carpenter who blows out his brains upon *Hamlet*. Only let him not blow out mine.

WHERE THE DRAMA IS ALIVE

These things being said for truth's sake, let me invite the reader to extol the performances in London of the Mansfield House Players, the Shoreditch Drama and the St. Pancras People's Theatre. The amateur movement is particularly strong in Yorkshire, in which county three of Shaw's plays, *Back to Methuselah*, *Heart-Break House*, and *Androcles and the Lion* were given in 1925 within a few weeks, the Sheffield Playgoers, the Sheffield Repertory Theatre and the Sheffield Educational Settlement being responsible. The Leeds Art Theatre, under the distinguished leadership of Miss Edith Craig, aims at producing the best in modern literary drama, and is said to be highly successful. The York Everyman

Theatre, under the leadership of Mr. Nugent Monk, aims at producing the best in literary drama of all periods, and its programme for 1926 ranges from a morality play and Webster's *The Duchess of Malfi* to Ernest Toller's *The Machine Wreckers*. The Huddersfield Thespians are the only good thing I have ever known to come out of Huddersfield. The Leeds Industrial Theatre was inaugurated by the Rev. Percival Gough, who encouraged his parishioners to perform scenes from the plays of Shakespeare. We are told that he "worked on the theory that drama was most valuable as a means of self-expression, and, therefore, interfered as little as possible between the play and the players, not even troubling to correct their speech or to tone down their dialect." The trouble, of course, begins when professional critics, bidden to such performances, work on the theory that criticism is most valuable as a means of expressing themselves and what they think about such performances. One insists again that the *entire value* of amateur performances of the drama lies in the benefit derived by the actors themselves and by their friends, and not in the amount of enjoyment their performance may afford a professional critic. This may very well be nil. It is undoubtedly good for the child next door to express itself in terms of Clementi's Sonatas, though enjoyment on this side of the wall may not accrue.

Lancashire and Cheshire are also rich in dramatic societies, and experts in amateur acting speak very highly of the Stockport Garrick Society, the Un-named Society, Manchester, and the Altrincham and Marple Garrick Societies. Coming south one arrives at the Maddermarket Theatre, Norwich, which has the advantage of a permanent theatre, direction by Mr. Nugent Monk, and the services of a charwoman and an electrician. The performances are said to be admirable. Other ventures of which mention must be made, though my scope does not permit detail, are Citizen House, Bath, The School of Dramatic Study at the East London College, the Liverpool University Dramatic Society, the Glastonbury Festival Movement, the Hardy Players, the Portmaddoc Players, the Stoneland Players, the Shoreham Village Players and the Village Drama Society. It is the existence of these Societies which encourage one to believe that all is well with the state of Denmark.

I am particularly anxious to avoid the charge of sneering at worthy and well-meant effort.

But to say that one does not derive enjoyment from a thing is not necessarily to sneer at it. Mind you, like Mr. Ramsden, "I have not read the book." I have not seen many of the societies named in action, but some little time ago I did see, in the north of England, a performance of a fine play by one of our finest minds. The society in question asked me to recommend a piece, which I did. They acted on my recommendation and there their acting ended. I was invited to witness the performance, which I did at the cost of two days and a considerable journey. I found that everybody engaged in the performance had sweated blood, doubtless doing themselves an immense amount of physical and intellectual good in the process. But as a piece of art or even entertainment the thing was null and void, possibly because the players obeyed too strongly the poet's command to "paint the soul, never mind the legs and arms." But that was the actors' affair; to the spectator it was obvious that only one person on the stage knew what to do with his hands. One would repeat, if necessary *ad nauseam*, that expertness and proficiency are not the measure of these enterprises which spring from a love of drama and a need for self-expression. Intention and not achievement is the test, and the critic who should do his duty by them must abrogate his one golden rule which is to judge by achievement and ignore intent. I have not the strength of mind to do this. I cannot pretend that a performance is not green because the actor is thinking in purple.

LOOKING FOR A MIRACLE

Yet I hold that it is in the hearts of the amateurs of England that the drama is flourishing. But that the theatre is dead even in town I would strongly deny; in the lesser city which is Shaftesbury Avenue it may be a sickly plant, but in those play-houses which are run by managers interested in play-producing apart from money-making, and in greater London, it blooms magnificently. Only three conditions are necessary to restore to pristine glory even the fashionable London theatre. The first will be achieved when the public learns to go to a good play betimes, and the second as soon as playwrights realise that there are other subjects in the world besides sex. The miracle will have happened in its entirety on the night when an author, called by an applauding house, shall advance to the foot-lights and say:

"LADIES AND GENTLEMEN:

"Whilst thanking you for the magnificent reception you have accorded to my play, I can only express my astonishment that you should not have hissed it. Seldom has a more talentless piece of hack-work been offered by an impecunious playwright to an uncritical public. Had you the brains to perceive it you would know that this piece, which has been written solely for gain, is impudently bad from start to finish. It is only because managers realise your lack of critical faculty, and authors are hard-up, that this worthless rubbish has been placed before you in the hope and conviction that your ignorance and stupidity will make it the usual phenomenal success."

AGATE, JAMES
A SHORT VIEW OF THE ENGLISH STAGE, 1900-1926.

DATE DUE

GAYLORD	PRINTED IN U.S.A.